THE
LIFE
AUDIT

•••••• A workbook for a healthier, happier you ••••••

THE
LIFE
AUDIT

MICHELLE MORONEY

GILL BOOKS

Gill Books

Hume Avenue

Park West

Dublin 12

www.gillbooks.ie

Gill Books is an imprint of M.H. Gill and Co.

© Michelle Moroney 2019

978 07171 8473 6

Designed by Tanya M Ross, elementinc.ie

Copy-edited by Djinn von Noorden

Printed by BZ Graf, Poland

Photos courtesy of unsplash.com. Author photo courtesy of @drishti_studio, drishtivideography.com

This book is typeset in Johnston light 8pt on 11pt

The paper used in this book comes from the wood pulp of managed forests. For every tree felled, at least one tree is planted, thereby renewing natural resources.

A CIP catalogue record for this book is available from the British Library.

5 4 3 2 1

To my parents, Tadg and Gaye.
For everything.

ACKNOWLEDGEMENTS

My sincere thanks and gratitude goes to you, the reader. Without a potential set of eyes and a pair of hands to take in this body of work it would never have manifested.

Secondly, thank you to every single person who showed up to practise and learn with me over the past 17 years. For your belief and trust in me I am privileged and honoured.

Thank you to my editor, Sarah Liddy, who stuck with me, and for our shared creative process which taught me that straight lines are not a part of our chemistry. To the whole team at Gill Books for their love and attention to this work; their professionalism in their mission to share educating and enlightening content is second to none.

To the wonderful team at the Cliffs of Moher Retreat, for believing in me, in what we do, and for being part of something special.

My parents, to whom I dedicate this book. Their unconditional love, constant support and unwavering belief in me has been the foundation for my whole journey, and to have them as my parents is the highest of blessings.

To my husband, who knows me better than most, loves me more than any, and allows me the room to grow. His deep roots in our relationship allow me to safely soar high.

Lastly, but most important, to my three beautiful boys who are my greatest teachers in life. They have cracked open my heart forever.

Contents

Introduction

THIS IS YOUR LIFE

This journey we are all on is a wondrous and extraordinary thing. It is challenging and beautiful, dull and adventurous, exciting and heartbreaking. It is all things at all times and navigating our way is anything but simple. There is no instruction and a lot of outer distraction. It can be intimidating and scary as well as fun and full of endless possibilities. This life is precious and fast and we all want to make the most of it.

THE COMMONALITY THAT UNITES US ALL

Facilitating retreats as I have done for over 15 years has given me the privilege of working with some of the bravest, most courageous and open-minded people I have ever met. People who take time out of their busy lives and away from their loved ones to do the Big Work. To ask the Big Questions. It doesn't seem to matter what age, nationality, stage of life or even what kind of life our guests have. The one desire that connects us all, and that stems from a deep knowing, is that we *can* feel better, we *can* have more energy, we *can* manage our feelings and our emotions better and we *can* see the world through fresh, positive eyes again. It was years of working with people before I would look around my circle of students and see that despite everyone looking different, sounding different and saying different things, we are all, in fact, the same.

Perhaps the voices in my head were so loud I couldn't hear it. Perhaps the lens through which I was viewing life was so caught up in my own story that I couldn't see it. But one day I looked around the circle of people that had shown up from all over the world to work, learn, practice and play with me at my retreat and I knew it was truth.

Yes, we are all unique and special with individual tastes, expressions and desires. Yes, we all have different backgrounds and histories and we all see, learn and experience the world in a distinctive way. Yet what I came to know and understand is that despite this, we feel the same pain. We suffer the same loss. We love with the same heart and we experience joy with the same wonder.

We are all doing our best. We are all navigating our way on this journey and we all yearn to be loved, to be really seen and heard and to make the most of this extraordinary life.

We all want to be happy. We all want to feel better. We all want to get the most out of life and we don't want anything of our own design holding us back.

Life can be complicated. There are so many aspects to this not-so-simple life and while we are caught in the cycle of day-to-day living it can be hard to discern between what's working for us and where we are getting stuck. We might not know what's holding us back but we know that something isn't right.

We have our health to take into consideration – our mental, physical and emotional wellness. There are the relationships we are a part of: family, friends and perhaps a significant other. There is our finances and career to address and then there is fun, learning, self-development and spirituality. So many fragments make up the whole and each of them takes up a portion of our time, energy and overall capacity. Each part of ourselves affects the whole, and to bring ourselves into balance we must be willing to take a long look at each part of our life. Then we can truly take stock, be honest and open and make concrete plans to move past blockages and in the direction of our choosing.

This book is for you if:

* You are ready to start making small but significant lifestyle changes and to take control of your own life.

* You feel that there is something missing from your life.

* You are tired of talking about change, thinking about change and feeling bad about not making changes, and are ready to simply get going.

* You are lacking in energy and inspiration or often feel stressed and unwell.

THE LIFE AUDIT

The dictionary definition of an audit is 'an official inspection of an organisation's accounts, typically by an independent body'.

Let's think of your accounts as the different parts of your life: your family, health, career or occupation, friends, money and your personal development. And let's not forget about fun, the things you do that make you happy.

This book is the independent body that is going to work with you to take stock of these areas of your life. We might find that some of your accounts are in order and well balanced and we can admire the good work you've done. We might find that some of your accounts are badly organised, unbalanced and need some reviewing.

What this book really offers is support as you begin your journey. Think of this journey as a self-guided expedition, and this book is your fully comprehensive guide book. A source of information and inspiration helping you to navigate your way. A place to make plans and create your own maps and somewhere to journal and review as you go.

Taking the first step is always the hardest, but you are strong, capable and brave and this book is your ally to take that step and walk the journey with you as you navigate your way from where you are to where you want to be.

Towards a life of health, happiness and love.

How to Use This Book

Being audited is no fun, but let's take a moment and recognise something important. If we want change; if we want to take control and live our best life possible, we need self-discipline. No one wants to talk about this, but it is the truth. It *is* difficult. There is no magic pill and no short cut. We need self-discipline.

But please – do not let this put you off. This is *your* life, and no matter what this journey entails it will not be boring, and every little step we take matters.

And you *are* ready; by even reading this book you have already taken a huge step.

Let's start this audit, let's pull out those accounts and get to the bottom of what's working well and what's not working just as well.

AS WE JOURNEY THROUGH THE YEAR THERE ARE THREE PARTS TO EACH MONTH: EXPLORE, CONTEMPLATE AND CREATE.

EXPLORE

This is where we will explore who we are by using a set of questions and tasks. The questions are designed to get you really thinking about what is important to you. Trust the process and follow your instincts. Commit the time to getting to know the deepest aspects of who you are. And enjoy this journey. You deserve it.

You might answer all the questions in one go or it might take you a month to complete them. You might find some of the questions more challenging than others. Find a pace that works for you. Don't rush.

Take your time when it comes to writing your answers to the big questions. Focus. Centre. Being honest with ourselves requires starting from a place of calm and relaxation. Sometimes our minds begin to think ahead, imagining a make-believe person, or people, who might one day read what we're writing. Remember: this work is only for you. It is by you and for you, and is for no one else.

Before you start answering the questions, commit to giving yourself some time and space for this exploratory process. These questions are meant to prompt you to think about parts of your life that you might not often think about. They are designed to be thorny and difficult.

Here are some tips to help you to find focus and to create a powerful vision:

* Find a quiet place without any distractions. Consider turning off your phone or putting it on silent.

* Commit to a period of time – 30 minutes a week, perhaps.

* Close your eyes and take a few deep breaths. Count an inhale of four and an exhale of eight. Take ten deep breaths like this, allowing your count to lengthen as you become more comfortable.

* Remember that this work is a positive step towards taking ownership of your life and finding direction that fits in with who you are, what you believe in and what brings you joy.

CONTEMPLATE

Each month features a series of themes and tools to accompany you on your journey. Written to inspire and motivate, these seek to enhance your path by sharing wisdoms that have been passed through the ages and that have personally helped me on my journey. I am excited to share them with you. They include practices, insights and knowledge to encourage you and complement the work you are doing.

Tips

This is the part of the book you can read on the bus on the way to work, or take to bed with you to read before going to sleep. Make notes if you find parts that inspire you. Consider some of the themes as you are filling in your questions in the Create section. I recommend using a notebook or a journal in conjunction with the Contemplate section, as there may be topics you'd like to write about in more detail. Perhaps you will also find some of the practical parts of this section inspiring and want to try certain ideas yourself. Having a notebook is a great way to record the things that speak to you directly and that you want to follow up on.

CREATE

This is where you will bring everything together and begin to accomplish your goals. Without action, the work cannot permeate into our lives, and it is in this part that we get to see and feel the shifts that are happening as a result of the work. This section is led by you and uses a practical and accessible format. It is the combination of the first two parts and will guide you to take the steps that are right for you.

Tips

This is the part for which you are most responsible. Now it is up to you to put this into action. SMART goals (detailed on p.59 in Month Two) are an excellent support. They will help break goals down into bite-sized chunks and allow you to achieve what you set out to do. This is the most exciting part of the journey. Succeeding in our goals, no matter how small they may be as we start off, is a great way to learn that anything is possible. Take ownership of your journey. You can do this! *Remember, start small.*

The process towards achieving a small goal is the same as it is for achieving a larger goal. You can practise on the small ones first. Use your 100 Tool on p. 53 in Month Two to inspire you in your goals and use your answers to the questions in the Contemplate sections to refine what's important to you.

WE HAVE EVERYTHING WE NEED

For the most part, we each know what it is we need to unlock our potential and live our best life. Whether we are stuck in a rut of having no energy, making poor food choices and avoiding exercise, or struggling with low self-esteem, we don't need to look outside ourselves for answers. Somewhere inside we know exactly what it is we need in order to have more energy and vitality, a clearer and more peaceful mind, and a healthier and stronger body.

Life can be hard – we are dealt cards that we cannot control, cards that will knock us for six and leave us reeling. Yet we also hold our own deck of cards and there are a lot of choices that we *can* make that have a massively positive impact on our lives.

MAKING THE TIME

Making time for ourselves – stepping off the pages of our busy lives and looking at our life from the outside in – is an essential reframing exercise that allows us to take control of what's not working as well as it could be. Slowing down and taking small steps each day in the direction of where we want to go will bring us a long way over the course of a year.

There is so much information out there and there are literally hundreds of books written on every subject I have included in this one: I should know, my book shelves are full of them! I wrote this book to help people find clear and useful information and to develop the tools to introduce small changes that may eventually lead to big ones. I want to make it simple because, in the end, the truth is always simple. Ultimately, I wrote this book for you. That it may help to show you the way back home. To who you really are. To your true self.

We are complicated, intricate beings with a body, mind and soul that each needs to be nurtured, nourished and taken care of in a different way. Although we have different parts, each is connected, and to fulfil that picture of a 'whole self' we must consider these wonderful and diverse fragments.

THINK OF THIS BOOK AS YOUR ACCOMPANIMENT ON A SELF-GUIDED JOURNEY TO A BETTER LIFE.

THIS IS YOUR JOURNEY

Ultimately it will be your own unique combination of focuses and practices, tailored to suit your individual needs, and developing over time as you grow, that will help you to find balance and harmony in life. As you ease your way onto a path of lifestyle changes that will address your body, your mind, your emotions and your deepest, higher self, you put into action a great plan for realising your full potential.

Please approach this plan not from a mindset of scarcity ('I am not enough') but from a place of abundance ('You are allowed to be both a masterpiece and a work of progress simultaneously' – Sophia Bush).

Because you are.

MONTH ONE
Self-Reflection

EXPLORE

Welcome to month one! This is our month of beginnings, a month where we want to be our 'best selves'. If you are starting this in January (and you don't have to!) it's the month where new gym membership numbers soar with fresh aspirations that will probably never be realised. It's the month of resolutions – a desperate word that somehow implies that we are not enough as we are.

Now don't get me wrong – this book is about making lifestyle changes that will help us to be happier, healthier and feel more vital. But we are aiming to do this by embracing who we are and working to enhance that. Not by looking at ourselves in the mirror and wanting to change what we see.

As one of my yoga teachers used to say: 'We are absolutely perfect in every single way, with room for improvements.'

LIFE IS LIKE RIDING A BICYCLE. TO KEEP YOUR BALANCE YOU MUST KEEP MOVING.

– Albert Einstein

THE WHEEL OF LIFE

The Wheel of Life is a tool that has been used to find direction for over a thousand years. It is a tool to help us to move forward. Imagine getting in a car and not knowing where you are going. The journey might be exciting at first, but eventually we would become tired and confused, driving around with no clear destination or direction.

The Wheel of Life provides us with a simple bird's-eye view of what is going on with the many facets of our lives, and by knowing this we can find a direction we want to focus on. We are complicated beings, and there are many parts of our life that make up the whole:

* We have the people we are close to – our family, friends and perhaps a significant other.

* We have our professional lives – what we do to earn money, and our finances.

* We have our health – physical, mental and emotional.

* We have our environment – where and how we live.

* Lastly, there is fun and self-development – what we do for recreation, leisure and to relax and how we are growing in the world.

We may have consciously or unconsciously focused on one or more areas but neglected the others. For example, by focusing on our career, we may have overlooked our family or friends and not spent enough time cultivating these relationships. Or perhaps our health has taken a hit by not making time for proper exercise, diet and rest.

HOLISTIC = WHOLE

Because we are holistic, whole beings, when one area of our life is suffering, this inevitably seeps into all the other areas too. Whether we realise it or not, when there is a kink in the wheel, it does not roll smoothly and there is no balance.

The key to the Wheel of Life is not to have a totally full wheel, a 5/5 perfect picture, but to have some semblance of balance across all the areas of our life. This requires striving for equilibrium, which means giving different parts different amounts of attention at different times.

We will use the Wheel of Life twice in this book. Once at the beginning, to get an overall view of what is working and not yet working, and to help us evaluate what we want to address first; and once at the end, to see how the process has provided a greater sense of balance across all areas of our life. Small changes are often all that is needed to bring us into better alignment and that is what we will work on during the course of this year.

HOW TO USE THE WHEEL OF LIFE

As we go through each section of the wheel, we will ask ourselves the following questions on these areas of our life:

1. On a scale of 1 to 5, how satisfied are you with this area of your life? (1 meaning not satisfied at all and 5 meaning completely satisfied.)

2. How did you arrive at this number?

3. What is missing for you in this area of your life?

4. What can you do to add value to this part or your life?

Wheel sections:

1. Purpose: Do I know and am I satisfied with my purpose in life?

2. Personal Development: Am I satisfied with my growth and self-development?

3. Health and Wellness: Am I satisfied with my health, body and mind?

4. Stress and Relaxation: Am I satisfied with how I manage stress?

5. Finance and Career: Am I satisfied with my job and the money I have?

6. Family/Significant Other: Am I satisfied with the love in my life within my inner circle?

7. Community and Friends: Am I satisfied with my social life?

8. Fun and Recreation: Am I satisfied with the amount of fun I have?

9. Spirituality: Am I satisfied with my spiritual life?

Fill in your wheel and answer the questions. Be as honest as you can. If you can't answer a question then leave it and come back to it another time. Once you've finished take a moment to see where you scored the least and lean into this. Your scores will help you to see clearly which areas of your life to focus on first. Perhaps the wheel has shown that you have scored low with finances; then this is something you need to focus on first by establishing what you need to do to improve this area of your life. If you are single and feel that you would like to meet someone then this is an opportunity to see what is holding you back. Each month we will focus on one of the areas of the Wheel of Life and give you the opportunity to explore each section in more detail.

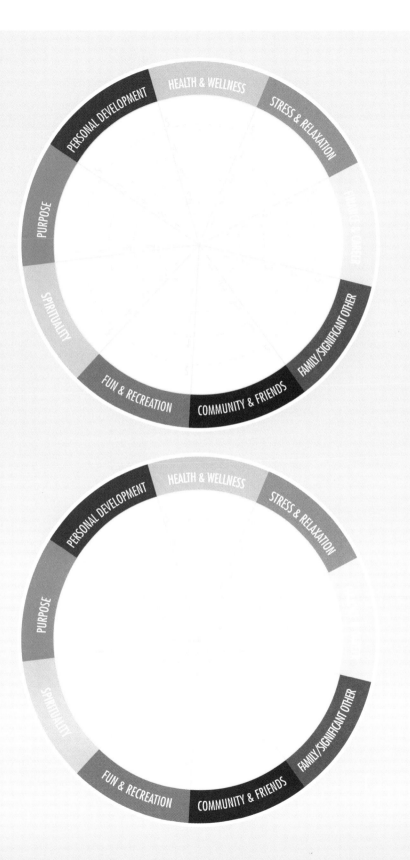

GAINING AN INSIGHT INTO WHO I AM, MY STRENGTHS, CAPABILITIES AND POTENTIAL

Describe yourself in six positive words:

1. _____

2. _____

3. _____

4. _____

5. _____

6. _____

What are your three greatest strengths?

1. _____

2. _____

3. _____

What are your top three skills?

1. _____

2. _____

3. _____

What are your three biggest successes in life to date?

1. _____

2. _____

3. _____

What comes easily to you?

1. _____

2. _____

3. _____

4. _____

Where do you bring the greatest value?

1. _____

2. _____

3. _____

4. _____

On a scale of 1–10, how happy are you with your life as it is now?

_____

_____

How did you reach this answer?

_____

_____

_____

_____

What do you have to bring to the world?

_____

_____

_____

_____

_____

_____

WE DON'T SEE THE WORLD AS IT IS,

WE SEE IT AS WE ARE.

– Anaïs Nin

WHAT ARE THE BEAUTIFUL THINGS
ABOUT YOU?

Spend some time thinking about this. Don't rush. Take your time. Fill a page. If you have more to say, fill your journal.

CONTEMPLATE

Listening

FINDING A LISTENING PARTNER

Having an ally on this journey can be really helpful. A friend or family member who gets you, honours and respects the work you are doing and who wishes to be a part of your journey. Setting up a symbiotic relationship with someone who can be there for you by listening to you, someone who can hold space for you to express when you need to express, can play a significant role on your path. It's important that you can offer the same for this person and there are a few guidelines to direct the focus of this relationship.

A note on confidentiality

Whatever gets said in a listening partnership must never be referred to again. Not to another person, nor to each other, either inside or outside of this setting. Once it is said, that is it. It is not spoken of again unless your partner carries the theme on again at another time. This is a safe space where anything can be said, and nothing shall be repeated. For example, during a listening session your partner refers to her mother being ill. If this is the only time she has shared this information with you, you do not ask after her mother outside of the listening session unless your partner brings it up herself.

Listening sessions

These can be done person to person or over the phone.

Person to person

* Meet in a place where you have privacy and can be undisturbed for the length of time you choose for the session. Put phones to silent or airplane mode. Decide on an amount of time per person – 5 minutes or 30 minutes, it's up to you. Set a timer.

* Start with one person talking and the other listening. It is important that the listener listens intently, with her eyes, body language and whole being. But the listener does not talk. Never. When the time has passed the person talking stops. It doesn't matter if they are mid-flow, the time is up.

* Take a few breaths together. The listener asks the talker a random question to bring them back to the moment, something simple like 'What is your favourite season?' – anything to bring them out of their flow. Change sides.

* Once the exercise is over, the listener asks another question. Take a few breaths. It's over.

Over the phone

This is done exactly the same way only over the phone. It works perfectly well as long as the protocol remains the same.

Voice messages

* In a busy world it can be challenging to make time to practise this often. Getting two people organised can be a challenge.

* Many apps have voice-message functions where you can record yourself talking and send the message to someone else. Mine even has a lock function so I don't have to hold a button down. I like to think of this as the modern equivalent of letter-writing. There is no pressure to respond or even to listen immediately. The sharer can talk when they feel the need and the listener can sit to *really* listen when they have the time. The effect is the same. Knowing that there is someone who cares, who will *really* hear us, has the same effect.

* It can take time to get used to articulating in this way, but it's a wonderful way to express and share. If you are worried about the content of your messages being saved or shared and at risk of others accidentally listening, you can request that your partner deletes them. An additional benefit is that you, the speaker, can listen back to your messages and gain insight into what's going on for you.

The benefits

Listening partnerships are a wonderful way to get out of our own head, especially when we are feeling reactive, angry or hurt. Having the space to say how we feel, and hearing it said out loud, can really help us to find clarity around our feelings. I often find I see different sides to a situation when I practice this. Sometimes I just rant, getting something off my chest that is heavy and needing to be said. Sometimes I express frustration with a relationship that I am not yet ready to discuss with the person in question.

> ONE OF OUR GREATEST NEEDS IS TO BE HEARD. WE CANNOT BE FIXED, NOR ARE WE SEEKING TO BE, BUT WE YEARN TO BE TRULY HEARD.

Many of us are carrying thoughts and feelings in our heads that we do not get to articulate. Once they come from the ethereal realm of the mind and into the physical realm of words, they often lose their charge and can be seen for what they are: longings, fears, worries, aspirations, dreams, noise, disappointments etc. We can see them; we can touch them. Speaking them can bring form and shape to the thoughts that created the feelings and emotions. We get to know ourselves, to know our minds.

We can allow it all to come out. The words we daren't say. We adore our loved ones; that doesn't mean they don't piss us off sometimes. We may not be able to express our feelings to the people who are bothering us, and indeed it is we who are annoyed/hurt/frustrated. Part of owning our own feelings is being able to identify them. Talking helps with this.

Our feelings are our feelings, right or wrong they may be. Our emotions are our emotions, whether they are fair or not. This is our chance to let it out, to say it all.

BEING VULNERABLE IN A SAFE SPACE IS HEALING.

BEING VULNERABLE IN AN UNSAFE SPACE IS TRAUMA.

We may not be getting this listening experience. We are surrounded by people, yet we may feel that no one is truly listening to us, allowing us to say whatever is on our minds and in our hearts, without judgement and without giving their opinion. This can apply in our home, social and work environments. It is nobody's fault; we are not trained to hold space like this. We were not taught it in school.

FIND IT.

SEEK IT OUT.

IT IS VITAL.

In the end, the real benefits come not from being the talker. The real magic of this work is becoming the listener.

IT IS HERE THAT THE GREATEST GROWTH OCCURS.

LISTENING WILL TEACH US ABOUT OURSELVES.

WE WILL BECOME OUR OWN TEACHER.

WE WILL START TO HEAL.

JOURNALING

The simple practice of journaling – yes, it's an actual verb – can create space in your mind and encourage your creative nature. Documenting our thoughts and feelings in writing has enormous benefits for our health. Some of these benefits include increased memory, the ability to manage stress and improvements in moods. A 2013 study on two groups scheduled for biopsies found that 76 per cent of adults who spent 20 minutes journaling for three days in a row, two weeks before the biopsies, were fully healed after 11 days, while 58 per cent of the control group had not yet recovered (https://www.ncbi.nlm.nih.gov/pubmed/23804013).

Think of journaling as having a kind and patient friend who is holding space for you to *literally* say anything you want. There is no limit, and no judgement.

We are complex beings and our thoughts and feelings are real to us, whether long term or moment to moment, whether actual or imagined, whether logical or irrational. How we feel is not always reasonable and doesn't always make sense. We react to situations not just at how they are presented in a given moment, but by how they make us feel in relation to our past experiences. The more unresolved our past traumas and experiences, the more likely they will rear up in moments of stress and discomfort in a bid to get us to notice, wake up and deal with them.

How people react to a challenge will vary greatly. For example, a cancelled flight can elicit extreme anger from one person and calmness from another, even when the consequences are worse for the latter. The reactions come from within and are coloured by our past. The angry person isn't simply responding to the current moment, she is responding from the place that the anger is masking.

Journaling is a gentle way to begin exploring these parts of ourselves. Writing is the act of bringing our thoughts to the surface and placing them into the physical realm. It is a momentous process.

Not only does giving our mind this opportunity to relieve itself of the chitter-chatter by allowing it to pour out like warm honey, thereby creating a calmer and more centred mind, it also allows space for pure and connected thought to emerge.

I JOURNAL MY JOY, AND MY JOY EXPANDS EXPONENTIALLY FOREVERMORE. SO BE IT.

– *Amy Leigh Mercree, Joyful Living: 101, Ways to Transform Your Spirit and Revitalize Your Life*

Getting to these places is difficult and messy. It takes courage to bring these thoughts out. We might find that we are constantly busy in a bid to hide from the very thoughts that we are now endeavouring to pour onto paper. Do not underestimate the power of taking these dark, ever-present thoughts and bringing them into the light of day. We might just find that they aren't as scary as we previously supposed, or that they aren't capable of causing as much pain as we imagined. Let it out. All of it. The sad, the scary, the judging, the criticising, the ugly, the hateful, the mean, the hurt, the lost, the scared and the unloved.

Security

The most important thing to know is that your private words are safe from anyone else's eyes – anyone's! This might require taking measures such as having a locked box in which to keep your journal. Or you might decide to ceremonially burn your daily thoughts, because that is *all* they are – the physical manifestation of the ramblings of our monkey mind. Some of the thoughts will be pure and deep and come from the infinite source of wisdom within; some will be pure crap. The key to this practice is that over time, as we grow more comfortable, relaxed and confident with our approach, we begin to discern between the gold and the crap.

Morning pages

Julia Cameron, in her book *The Artist's Way*, details a simple format that has helped unblock many creatives. She calls it the 'Morning Pages' and all over the world, people arise to this practice and report numerous benefits. She suggests writing three pages, longhand with a pen or pencil. The reasoning behind not doing it digitally is the ease at which we can delete and rewrite. The point of this exercise is to let flow whatever comes up, not to think about who might read it in the future, including ourselves, and to not edit as we go. If we think too carefully about what we are writing, then the exercise becomes something else.

Three pages of anything. If you don't know what to write, simply write 'I don't know what to write' over and over again until something else comes up. The magic is in the lengthy process: at some point during the three pages we find a flow from somewhere deeper than the initial busy mind.

I started doing this and immediately noticed the benefits throughout the rest of my day. I felt calmer, more present, better able to handle situations. On any given day where I didn't start with Morning Pages, I felt the difference with less presence of mind. It feels like a safe outlet to pour out my deepest, darkest thoughts as well as

JOURNAL WRITING IS A VOYAGE TO THE INTERIOR.

– Christina Baldwin

my flippant observations and irritations. I can detail my dreams. Sometimes I mull over a problem. I allow myself the freedom to hop from pillar to post, and also to stay on one subject. It doesn't matter. What's important is just doing it.

HOW I BEGIN

On the top of the page I write 'Morning Pages' and the date. The next line I write is 'This is going to be the best day ever'. Cheesy, yes. It's working out well for me. I write down my dreams, or what I can remember of them. Then I take a moment to think of something that I am grateful for. It's easy for me to always refer to the big things, my healthy happy family etc., but I try to think of something new or different so I'm not rewriting the same thing every day. Today I wrote that I am grateful for the birdsong outside my window and the lovely lie-in I had when I ignored my alarm clock and decided to get an extra hour of sleepy cuddles with my youngest child instead.

Then I reflect on something positive that happened the day before, and feel gratitude for it as I write the words. Then I set a positive intention for the day ahead. Something that I want to do or how I would like the day to roll. Then I freestyle.

THREE PAGES.

EVERY MORNING.

IT TAKES ME BETWEEN 25 AND 35 MINUTES.

CREATE

Listening partner

Find a listening partner, someone who is interested in doing this with you. Set up the protocol as per the notes on p. 20. Begin the process by either meeting up or leaving a message where you are speaking from the heart.

Start a journaling practice

Writing down your thoughts and feelings will enhance your journey and be a valuable addition to this book. You might decide to write your journal in the morning or evening, or else to write as you go. Having that place to document your feelings will help you to make sense of them. Commit to a month and see if it is helpful. Treat yourself to a beautiful diary that is just for you, something that can fit in your bag or that looks nice on your bedside locker.

MONTHLY REVIEW

What insights has the Wheel of Life given you about your life? Sum them up in one paragraph.

_____

_____

_____

_____

_____

_____

Which areas are you excited to work on?

_____

_____

_____

_____

Which areas of your life are giving you the most worry and concern?

_____

_____

_____

_____

MY NOTES

MY NOTES

MY NOTES

MY NOTES

MY NOTES

MY NOTES

MONTH TWO
My Purpose

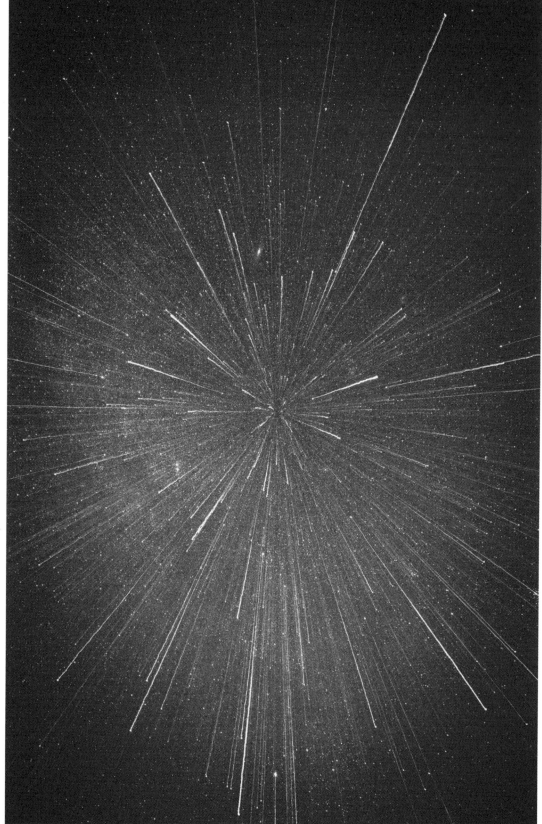

EXPLORE

Welcome to Month Two. In this chapter we will explore what brings you alive and what drives and inspires you. We will explore ways to creatively learn more about what makes you tick. The Contemplate section of this chapter has two parts, headed 'Finding your "Why"' and 'On procrastination'. The first section explores the what, why and how of finding our purpose and the second gives tools to help us to get there. These two work together: one helps us to know what we *want*, and the other helps us to *get* there. I hope they are useful for you.

THE MYSTERY
OF HUMAN
EXISTENCE LIES
NOT IN JUST
STAYING ALIVE,
BUT IN FINDING
SOMETHING TO
LIVE FOR.

– Fyodor Dostoyevsky

Understanding what motivates me

What makes me come alive?

_____

_____

_____

What is most important to me in my life and why?

_____

_____

_____

If I were facing into a month alone, what would I focus on?

_____

_____

_____

What am I most passionate about?

_____

_____

_____

What global causes am I passionate about? Which one is closest to my heart and why?

_____

_____

_____

Place the following values in order of importance:

HONESTY • CONSISTENCY
OPEN-MINDEDNESS • COMMITMENT
LOYALTY • RELIABILITY
DEPENDABILITY • COMPASSION
RESPECT • MOTIVATION
OPTIMISM • PASSION

_____

_____

_____

Take your top three values and write about your relationship with them. Why are they important to you?

_____

_____

_____

_____

_____

_____

THE PURPOSE OF LIFE IS A LIFE OF PURPOSE.

– Robert Byrne

CONTEMPLATE

Finding your 'Why'

Finding your purpose or 'Why' is a huge step in getting to know yourself better. In many ways it is the essence of this book and a natural outcome of doing the work. It's worth exploring as a concept as it can help us understand ourselves better.

What is our 'Why'?

Our 'Why' is at the very core of who we are and refers to our authenticity. Our 'Why' is what drives us, motivates us, is part of the choices and decisions we make and is at the heart of who we are. It is what we believe on the deepest level. It is what makes us different from everyone else.

Living an authentic life

Authenticity is when we do what we say and what we believe. In other words, when our actions are misaligned with what we say and what we believe, then we are not being authentic. For example, I believe deeply that connection to nature is fundamentally important to health and this is something I talk about in my classes. If I am not practising this myself, I am not being authentic. When I am not being authentic then I am vulnerable to outer influences and the risk of not being true to myself.

If there is no authenticity attached to our actions, we might find we are drifting or have a sense of unexplained dissatisfaction. We are simply moving though the world, acting and reacting to what is happening around us as it comes up.

Why find our 'Why'?

Making time to think about what our 'Why' is is a powerful step towards living a more authentic life. Focusing our intention on our 'Why' helps us to know ourselves better.

Authenticity is integrity at the highest level. It means we are being honest with ourselves first, honouring what is important to us. As this is coming from our core, we cannot but radiate this out into all areas of our life. We therefore have more integrity in our life as a result of knowing who we are on a deep level. We are more likely to do our best in any situation, even though our best will look different from day to day, moment to moment, depending on where we are or what is going on for us. But it will be our best, and that is integrity.

A YEAR FROM NOW YOU MAY WISH YOU HAD STARTED TODAY.

– Karen Lamb

THE REALLY
HAPPY PEOPLE
ARE THOSE WHO
HAVE BROKEN
THE CHAINS OF
PROCRASTINATION,
THOSE WHO FIND
SATISFACTION
IN DOING THE
JOB AT HAND.
THEY'RE FULL OF
EAGERNESS, ZEST,
PRODUCTIVITY.
YOU CAN BE, TOO.

– Norman Vincent Peale

Living in accordance with our core beliefs, knowing what they are and choosing to live a life committed to this, is an enlightened and spiritual path. We experience more serendipity and more synchronicity and this gives us a greater sense of trust in life. We find that there is a sense of flow to our life; for example, with the people with whom we come into contact and the experiences we have. Like pieces of a puzzle coming together, things start to make sense. We have a greater sense of clarity around what is important and what is not.

As we live in greater harmony with these beliefs, we find we have more passion for life, a sense that we are doing what we are meant to do. This sense of purpose fuels us, cuts through the haze and gives us more energy.

A LIFE LIVED WITH CLEAR PURPOSE AND INTENTION IS A LOT EASIER TO BE GRATEFUL FOR THAN ONE THAT IS NOT. IT IS ALSO A LOT MORE FUN.

HOW TO FIND YOUR 'WHY'

Part of the intention of this book is to discover this. Using the questions, journaling your thoughts, reading the content in each chapter and taking action with the exercises will help and inspire you to get to know yourself on a deeper level.

Some of the questions will explore the things you love and what comes easy to you. Some will question what qualities you enjoy expressing in the world. Others will get you thinking about where you are, where you want to be and will help you to prepare for a journey.

> WE DON'T KNOW WHAT WILL HAPPEN ON OUR JOURNEY, BUT AS LONG AS WE KNOW OUR DESTINATION, HAVE A ROAD MAP AND SOME PROVISIONS, WE *WILL* GET THERE.

On procrastination

A big word, a bigger problem. Five little syllables and a lifetime of denial. Why is it that the things that are most important to us, that are the most beneficial in our growth and development, are the very things that we resist the most? We are not alone in this: it is a blight that affects us all and chances are that this idea is familiar to you on a deep level.

In his inspiring book, *The War of Art*, Steven Pressfield calls out resistance as the enemy, and claims that the more important something is for our growth and personal development, the more resistance we have towards it.

I have experienced it over and over again. I experienced it this morning. I woke tired and groggy and despite having an arrangement to meet a friend at 7 a.m. for a cold dip in the Atlantic, upon rising I listened to my mind make excuse after excuse until there was no time left to cancel. I reluctantly made my way to the shore. I have swum in the early morning hundreds of times, and have first-hand knowledge that the ocean will give me everything I need.

I go in tired, blue and deflated. I emerge ALIVE. I *want* to feel good, victorious, strong, ready. I have kids to get to school, food to make, work to do.

But there it was, resistance. Not even trying to hide, resistance shouting in my face so emboldened it didn't even try to disguise itself. *Cancel. Message her.* There wasn't even time for me to go back to bed. There was nothing to gain by not going and everything to lose. Resistance was there, despite the two and a half years of daily sea swims, despite the cellular knowledge of the benefits, despite the need to feel better. What I've come to learn is that resistance will always be there. But I don't have to consent to it.

Today I didn't. Right up to the moment when I met my friend on the promenade it was there. But I did it anyway. The ocean wove her magic on me and I walked back up the beach with a sparkle in my eye and a spring in my step. Resistance: 0. Me: 1.

The learning for me was *knowing* that the resistance was there. By feeling and acknowledging and by not denying it, I was able to overcome it. It will be there again in some form. Some days less, some days more.

RESISTANCE WILL BE THERE. DO IT ANYWAY.

I BELIEVE IN THE RESISTANCE AS I BELIEVE THERE CAN BE NO LIGHT WITHOUT SHADOW; OR RATHER, NO SHADOW UNLESS THERE IS ALSO LIGHT.

– *Margaret Atwood,* The Handmaid's Tale

Here is the truth. On a path to a more balanced life with a healthy body, mind and emotions, there is work to do. There isn't a magic pill we can take to be happy; there isn't one practice that will give us what we desire. We need willpower, we need self-belief and we need self-discipline.

Even the word 'discipline' can make us recoil. It is a word often associated with naughty children or miserly living with a lack of colour and joy. But we can learn so much from the great sages of the past who in their own lifetime acquired enlightenment. Their insights manifested as a deep sense of peace, and they revealed dedication, commitment and self-discipline as the method to finding it.

DISCIPLINE IS FEELING RESISTANCE AND DOING IT ANYWAY. DOING IT ANYWAY IS STARTING SMALL: RUNNING ONE MILE, NOT COMMITTING TO RUNNING A MARATHON.

Think about the subtle ways you might demonstrate resistance:

* An 'all-or-nothing' mindset that means not trying new things.
* Waiting for the circumstances or conditions to be perfect.
* Dropping a goal because we failed at one small step.
* Blaming another person for what we didn't/cannot do.
* Blaming our work/family/commitments for not doing something.
* Finding excuses.
* Succumbing to procrastination.

In the words of Steven Pressfield, it's time to turn pro; to become a professional in your own life. Allowing procrastination to prevail by letting resistance hold you back from the greatness you are capable of, from living the life you were created for – that's being an *amateur* in your own life. It's time to turn pro at living *your* best life. To confront resistance and take small steps towards those very things that make you feel alive, that bring you joy and that fill you with a sense of purpose and destiny.

It isn't easy. Resistance is strong, smart and convincing and the closer we come to succeeding the fiercer it becomes. We don't have to beat it. We just have to stay disciplined enough to take that one step.

THEN THE NEXT.

THEN THE NEXT.

THAT IS ALL. THAT IS ENOUGH.

CREATE

The 100 Tool

The 100 Tool is a great way to think about what you want, what you *think* you want, and to ascertain what your priorities really are.

How to use this tool

Make a list of a hundred things that you would like to achieve in your lifetime. You don't have to write them in one go; take as long as you like. It might seem a mammoth task, but it is the process of writing that gives us a glimpse into what's important for us and what our dreams are. Your goals can be anything that is important for you, for example, spending more time in nature, reading a particular book, learning to play the piano, mending a relationship, hiking Machu Picchu, visiting Omey Island, and so on.

Let your creativity go wild and write whatever comes to mind. Life is not simply a set of goals to be achieved in order to be content. This is not the key to happiness. But in doing this activity we are seeking to find what makes us tick, what brings us joy, what is important for us and what we are looking for in our life.

Beside each goal, write down how important it is, giving it a score of 1 to 10, with 1 being incredibly important and 10 being not at all important. This is a great opportunity to see that some goals do not take precedence anymore, although they may once have been important. Some will still be significant, but as we grow and evolve, so too do our priorities. We get to see our true desires versus our list of 'shoulds' or past dreams that we are still holding onto and haven't given ourselves the opportunity to let go of.

View and review

Keep this list on you and refer to it often. We can use this list as we progress through the book, drawing inspiration from it to bring action and direction into our lives.

Sometimes the smallest goals can give us the biggest breakthrough and seeing how much progress you're making can be a great way to feel positive about what you *are* accomplishing. It will also give you the opportunity to re-evaluate the order of importance as this may change during the process.

THE 100 TOOL

Achievement		Importance
1. _____		_____ **/10**
2. _____		_____ **/10**
3. _____		_____ **/10**
4. _____		_____ **/10**
5. _____		_____ **/10**
6. _____		_____ **/10**
7. _____		_____ **/10**
8. _____		_____ **/10**
9. _____		_____ **/10**
10. _____		_____ **/10**
11. _____		_____ **/10**
12. _____		_____ **/10**
13. _____		_____ **/10**
14. _____		_____ **/10**
15. _____		_____ **/10**
16. _____		_____ **/10**
17. _____		_____ **/10**
18. _____		_____ **/10**
19. _____		_____ **/10**
20. _____		_____ **/10**
21. _____		_____ **/10**
22. _____		_____ **/10**
23. _____		_____ **/10**
24. _____		_____ **/10**
25. _____		_____ **/10**

THE 100 TOOL

Achievement	Importance
26.	/10
27.	/10
28.	/10
29.	/10
30.	/10
31.	/10
32.	/10
33.	/10
34.	/10
35.	/10
36.	/10
37.	/10
38.	/10
39.	/10
40.	/10
41.	/10
42.	/10
43.	/10
44.	/10
45.	/10
46.	/10
47.	/10
48.	/10
49.	/10
50.	/10

THE 100 TOOL

Achievement	Importance
51.	/10
52.	/10
53.	/10
54.	/10
55.	/10
56.	/10
57.	/10
58.	/10
59.	/10
60.	/10
61.	/10
62.	/10
63.	/10
64.	/10
65.	/10
66.	/10
67.	/10
68.	/10
69.	/10
70.	/10
71.	/10
72.	/10
73.	/10
74.	/10
75.	/10

THE 100 TOOL

Achievement	Importance
76.	/10
77.	/10
78.	/10
79.	/10
80.	/10
81.	/10
82.	/10
83.	/10
84.	/10
85.	/10
86.	/10
87.	/10
88.	/10
89.	/10
90.	/10
91.	/10
92.	/10
93.	/10
94.	/10
95.	/10
96.	/10
97.	/10
98.	/10
99.	/10
100.	/10

TRUST THE
PROCESS.
YOUR TIME
IS COMING.
JUST DO THE
WORK AND
THE RESULTS
WILL HANDLE
THEMSELVES.

– Tony Gaskins

SMART GOALS

Many of my journeys didn't start simply. Many of my journeys began with unrealistic expectations and unachievable goals. Needless to say, many of my journeys never got anywhere.

So many times, I started a health plan or a new practice with an all-or-nothing approach. Whether this was to exercise more, eat better or start a daily meditation practice, I set myself up to fail before I even began with unachievable goals. I know I'm not alone in experiencing this and the idea of change can be so intimidating that many of us don't get off the starting block. In addition to unrealistic goals, I used to make the mistake of confusing the goal with the actual steps. Or I would fail at a step and then give up on my goal.

For example, I decided that I would get up early every morning and practise yoga for 90 minutes. The first morning I turned off the alarm and went back to sleep. The second morning I turned off the alarm and went back to sleep. The third morning I got up, went to my mat exhausted and didn't enjoy my practice, so went back to bed and back to sleep. I gave up.

My goal was to practise yoga. But with the unrealistic addition of 'every morning for 90 minutes', once I failed at that I totally let go of the original goal. Breaking my goal down into smaller steps made it more achievable. *I will practise yoga for 20 minutes, three mornings a week.* Much more realistic, much more achievable. If I missed one, it was OK. I could make it up. Failing at a step does not mean giving up on a goal.

The key is to firstly figure out *what* you want. Once you're clear on the 'what', move on to the 'how'. The most useful tool I know to getting anything done is to turn what we want into a SMART goal.

A SMART GOAL IS:

SPECIFIC

MEASURABLE

ACHIEVABLE

REALISTIC

TIME-BOUND

For example, let's say we want to start the day with a glass of warm lemon water and continue to hydrate well for the rest of the day. Here is a SMART goal around that.

Specific: Drink lemon water in the morning and hydrate well throughout the day with seven glasses of water or herbal tea.

Measurable: Drink one glass of lemon water upon waking at 7 a.m., one on arrival into work at 9 a.m. and one at 11 a.m. One at lunch at 1 p.m. One at 3 p.m. and one before leaving work at 5 p.m. Drink one with dinner and a cup of herbal tea before going to bed.

Achievable: Yes. Work has a water filter and I will bring a large glass with me.

Realistic. Yes.

Time-bound: I will start this on Monday 7 January and continue for a month until Thursday 31 January and will review then.

This is a relatively easy plan. It is specific and most importantly it has a time frame for reviewing it. The time frame can be shorter if you're not sure whether the plan is realistic and achievable. You might decide on week one, after which you can determine whether it was too ambitious or not ambitious enough and make any changes and start again.

It takes anywhere between one and three months to really form a habit and so keeping this up, with hydration, for example, will eventually form a habit after which a SMART goal is no longer needed. At that point proper hydration is simply a part of your life and your focus and energy can go elsewhere.

Most importantly, you will have achieved so much by succeeding at your goal and will be full of confidence that you can make positive changes to your life with ease. In the same way, small, slow changes have a massive impact on our life so we do not need to approach change with an all-or-nothing mentality. Phew.

SMART GOALS WORKSHEET

SMART goals are designed to help you identify whether what you want to achieve is realistic and to determine a deadline. When writing SMART goals, use concise language, but include relevant information. They are designed to help you succeed, so be positive when answering the questions. Use your journal to keep track of your SMART goals.

INITIAL GOAL	Write the goal that you have in mind:
S SPECIFIC	• What do you want to accomplish? • Who needs to be included? • When do you want to do this? • Why is this a goal?
M MEASURABLE	• How can you measure progress and know if you've successfully met your goal?
A ACHIEVABLE	• Do you have the skills required to achieve the goal? • If not, can you obtain them? What is the motivation for this goal? • Is the amount of effort required on par with what the goal will achieve?
R REALISTIC	• Is it realistic? • Is it aligned with my overall objectives?
T TIME-BOUND	• What's the deadline?
SMART GOAL	Review what you have written and craft a new goal statement based on what the answers to the above questions have revealed.

MONTHLY REVIEW

What was the take-home from this month?

_____

_____

_____

_____

_____

_____

_____

List three things that you are inspired to begin after this month.

1. _____

2. _____

3. _____

List the top five things on your 100 Tool that excite you the most.

1. _____

2. _____

3. _____

4. _____

5. _____

MY NOTES

MY NOTES

MY NOTES

MY NOTES

MY NOTES

MY NOTES

MONTH THREE
Self-Development

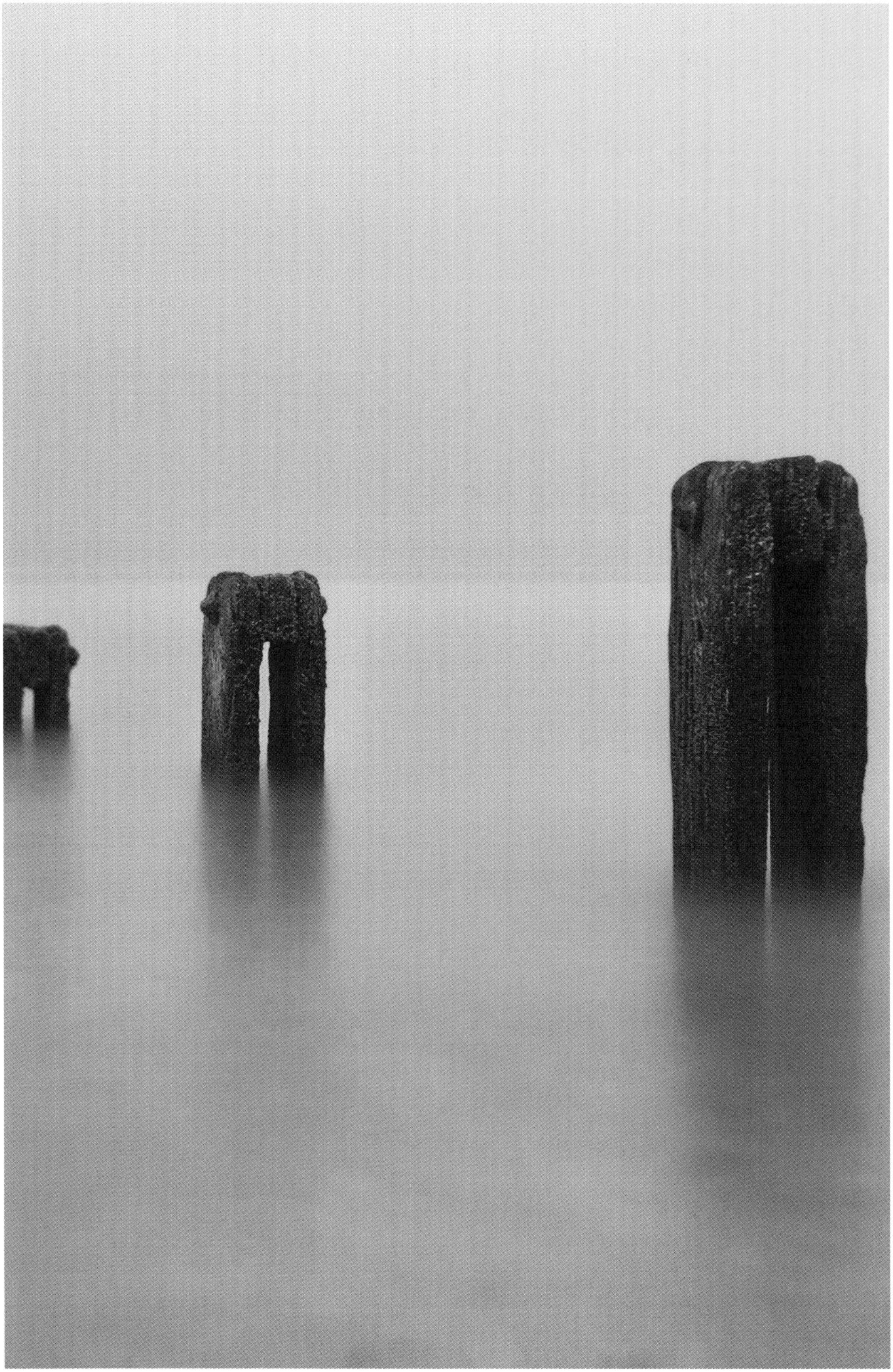

EXPLORE

Welcome to Month Three. I hope you are enjoying the process so far and that the journey is starting to unfold for you. We've explored who we are, what we believe in and what makes us happy in the last two chapters. Now we are going to explore self-growth and taking responsibility for our life and our actions. We will look at what is holding us back from self-growth and examine where some of these blockages may be coming from. We will explore two great themes that can help us to be more of who we are, and not allow things to get in our way. The first refers to our boundaries and knowing what is enough and what is too much. The second delves into gratitude and explores this practice as a tool for growth and self-development. I hope that you find these sections useful.

Consider the following questions:

Are you where you want to be in terms of personal growth?

_____

_____

_____

Have you accomplished everything you thought you would have by now?

_____

_____

_____

Is your life one of your choosing?

_____

_____

_____

If not, then who is choosing it for you?

_____

_____

_____

How are you growing as a person?

_____

_____

_____

If you knew you were going to die one year from today, what would you do with the time you had left? (Don't rush.)

_____

_____

_____

What has been the biggest challenge in your life to date?

_____

_____

_____

What has been the most difficult challenge in the past three years?

_____

_____

_____

What major changes have you faced over the past five years?

_____

_____

_____

Name five things that you are putting up with right now.

1. _____

2. _____

3. _____

4. _____

5. _____

What are your deepest fears?

_____

_____

_____

_____

If you weren't scared, what would you do?

_____

_____

_____

_____

What is true about you today that would make your eight-year-old self cry?

_____

_____

_____

_____

What's enough and what's too much?

This may seem like a simple-enough philosophy, but the balance between the two can be unquestionably difficult to find. 'Busy' is a problem for most of us, whether you have a demanding job, a hectic social life, a family to mind, are caring for others or all the above.

How we see the world, and act and react to it, is defined not just from the present situation, but from past experiences. We bury pain to forget it. Examples of this include becoming a workaholic, anaesthetising ourselves with alcohol and drugs or keeping frantically busy all the time. The last one might not appear as damaging, but it is important to address. Doing things for others can be disguised as altruism, selflessness even, but not making enough time to solve our own problems first makes our philanthropy less potent.

BEFORE WE BEGIN THIS PROCESS OF CREATING POSITIVE LASTING LIFESTYLE CHANGES, WE NEED TO MAKE SPACE.

KNOWING WHAT IS ENOUGH AND WHAT IS TOO MUCH AND THEN SAYING NO IS A GREAT PLACE TO START.

THE LITTLE THINGS?
THE LITTLE MOMENTS?
THEY AREN'T LITTLE.

– Jon Kabat-Zinn

HOW WE DO ANYTHING, IS HOW WE DO EVERYTHING.

To get to the bottom of this we must first find out what speed we are going at.

Are you an all-or-nothing person? Are you hard on yourself? What is your inner critic tuned to? A good time to find out is when we are doing something challenging – an exercise class, challenging yoga session, a run, a deadline, a public performance.

Is your critic standing on the sideline, cheering you on? Or is the voice in your head telling you that you're not good enough? When we are challenged and doing something out of the ordinary, we get an insight into our inner voice.

I was shocked when I first realised that my inner critic was tuned to criticism and that the voice in my head wasn't cheering but judging me. I am a kind and compassionate person who extends kindness and compassion to my friends and family. Yet, here I was, issuing the opposite to myself.

During a challenging class I was comparing myself to others, to my former self, to the yoga teacher. I wasn't practising for where I was in that moment, honouring my body and my energy levels that vary so much day by day, moment by moment. Yet here was a woman, a mother who wasn't getting much sleep, who was breastfeeding and providing sustenance for another, who showed up, and who was moving and breathing and doing her best.

It was suddenly obvious to me that *I should* be cheering for myself. It was a painful and life-changing revelation. The voice had been singing this song for so long that I could no longer hear it. *Until I actually stopped and actively listened.* I have since changed the narrative of my inner critic. It isn't always easy and that self-doubt still raises its head occasionally, but I am much kinder to myself. Also, I frequently take rest breaks during yoga classes.

Are you willing to explore your inner critic and find out what she is tuned to?

The next time you are challenged, stop to listen. That voice has been in there a long time and it takes refinement and coming back to the intention over and over again – but with patience we will hear it again.

Write about it. And then change *your* narrative.

Saying No

This is a hard one for many of us. Unless you are a wise and badass soul who knows instinctively what's enough and what's too much, you might find this word difficult.

Many of us feel the need to please, to be nice and to keep other people happy. This all sounds very noble until we are suddenly overburdened. We are often juggling so many red-hot knives in the air at one time that there simply isn't enough room to breathe.

Saying no might be the one move we can make that can really help us.

WHEN WE SAY NO TO SOMETHING, WE ARE SAYING YES TO SOMETHING ELSE.

It doesn't have to be a rude, outright no. We can pad it out and phrase it like this: 'Thank you for considering me for this, but unfortunately I'm not able to participate this time.'

Buying time is another useful way to not saying yes immediately: 'Thank you for considering me for this. I'll have a think about it and get right back to you.' Or: 'I'm delighted to be asked. I'd like to think about it and I will get back to you soon.'

In fact, if you have a hard time saying no, memorise the sentences above and you'll never be caught off-guard again. And if you're not looking after yourself because you're looking after the needs of so many others, who's going to look after them when you are burned out?

No is a tool. No matter how challenging it is, it might be life-saving. Think about the last time you agreed to something that you didn't want to do. How did it make you feel? Why didn't you say no? What would you like to say no to a bit more in your life?

GRATITUDE

Gratitude is a practice. The more we are grateful for the abundance we have, the more abundance we attract. The more time we spend focusing on what we do not have, what we do not want or what we do not like, the more we end up attracting. It's a simple law, and it works – regardless of whether we are paying attention to it or not.

The practice of gratitude has been widely researched and its benefits have been proven to make us happier and healthier and mentally and emotionally stronger. It creates empathy and reduces aggression. It improves low self-esteem and increases energy levels.

A number of years ago the idea that such a simple practice could produce such huge benefits might have sounded either far-fetched or cultish, but with the rise of depression and mental health challenges a lot of attention has been brought to this simple practice. Gratitude journals are available in most bookshops and many of the world's leading inspirational and motivation teachers are shouting from the rooftops about how this simple practice has transformed their lives.

How do we become more grateful?

For me it started with the small things. Much as how religious people say grace before a meal, I started to feel regular gratitude for simple things. Grateful for a safe journey home in the car. Grateful for a beautiful sunset. Grateful for a cup of tea.

Humility

Humility is the sister quality to gratitude. When we are present in the moment and feeling gratitude, we are also connecting to humility.

Humility means becoming aware of how sacred, special and beautiful our existence is.

Humility means understanding and embracing our love for others and the reciprocated love back at us.

Humility means marvelling at the beauty and perfection of nature.

When we connect to this feeling, we know that everything is as it should be and we feel at one with the world. Humility is the quality of wisdom and perception. Gratitude and humility create a powerful energy that can create the most beautiful of settings and destroy the most powerful of egos.

YOUR 'VIBRATION' IS A FANCY WAY OF DESCRIBING YOUR OVERALL STATE OF BEING. EVERYTHING IN THE UNIVERSE IS MADE UP OF ENERGY VIBRATING AT DIFFERENT FREQUENCIES. EVEN THINGS THAT LOOK SOLID ARE MADE UP OF VIBRATIONAL ENERGY FIELDS AT THE QUANTUM LEVEL. THIS INCLUDES YOU.

– *Cassandra Sturdy*

CREATE

Gratitude journaling

Taking it a step further is to write it down. Either make a section in your journal or get a new journal especially for this. Each day when you wake up, write down three things that you are grateful for in life.

As a mother of three gorgeous boys it would be very easy for me to write how grateful I am for them every day. But I would just be repeating myself. Try to get creative and to extend it out into all the different parts of your life. The more you practise this, the easier it will flow. Give it time.

If you want to do a follow-on practice, before you go to bed write down three wonderful things that happened that day. Again, they can be big things or small things, but taking the time to acknowledge the good things, especially during a tough day, has a powerful effect as we end the day.

When you've finished your writing, take a moment to read what you have written and to breathe into the gratitude. Seek to feel this gratitude in your body and in your breath. It is more than just words. It is a sensation and an energy. It is a vibration.

When we vibrate on this frequency, one of gratitude, feeling it in our minds and in our bodies, that is how we attract more of what we want into our life.

GRATITUDE MEDITATION

A short, five-minute meditation to begin cultivating gratitude.

Instructions:

1. Find a comfortable seat.

2. Set a timer for a period of time. Start with five minutes and increase only if it feels natural to as the days go by.

3. Place your hands over your heart centre, one over the other.

4. Begin to flip through the pages of your life, finding all that you have to be grateful for today.

5. Start with people. Run through them one by one, honouring and feeling the gratitude for their presence in your life.

6. Continue to the opportunities you have. Run through them one by one, offering gratitude for each.

7. See if you can feel the gratitude as a physical feeling. It may not happen straight away. Tune in to how your body feels as you practise this. You may start to feel a warmth or a tingling in your chest, or something else. Sit with this. Lean into it.

8. Continue.

9. As your mind wanders, gently bring it back to the task.

10. Continue, working your way through your life.

11. Take a moment to acknowledge the smaller things: a smile from a stranger, a ray of light through the clouds.

12. Feel this sensation of gratitude growing in your chest and expanding to fill you. Become aware that your whole body is resonating with the sensation of gratitude. Visualise the gratitude as a physical sensation and a bright light that is shining out through the tips of your fingers, down through your toes and out of the crown of your head.

MONTHLY REVIEW

Write down how many times you practised the gratitude meditation. How many times did you explore gratitude this month?

_____

_____

_____

_____

_____

_____

_____

Write down all the things that you are grateful for in your life; the people, opportunities, anything at all. See just how many things you can add to the list.

_____

_____

_____

_____

_____

_____

_____

_____

MY NOTES

MY NOTES

MY NOTES

MY NOTES

MY NOTES

MY NOTES

MONTH FOUR
Health and Wellness

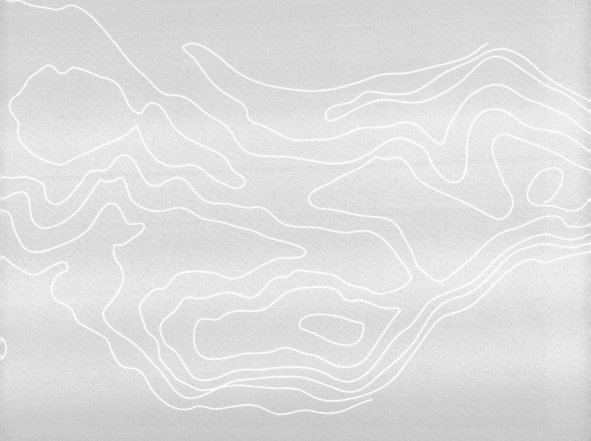

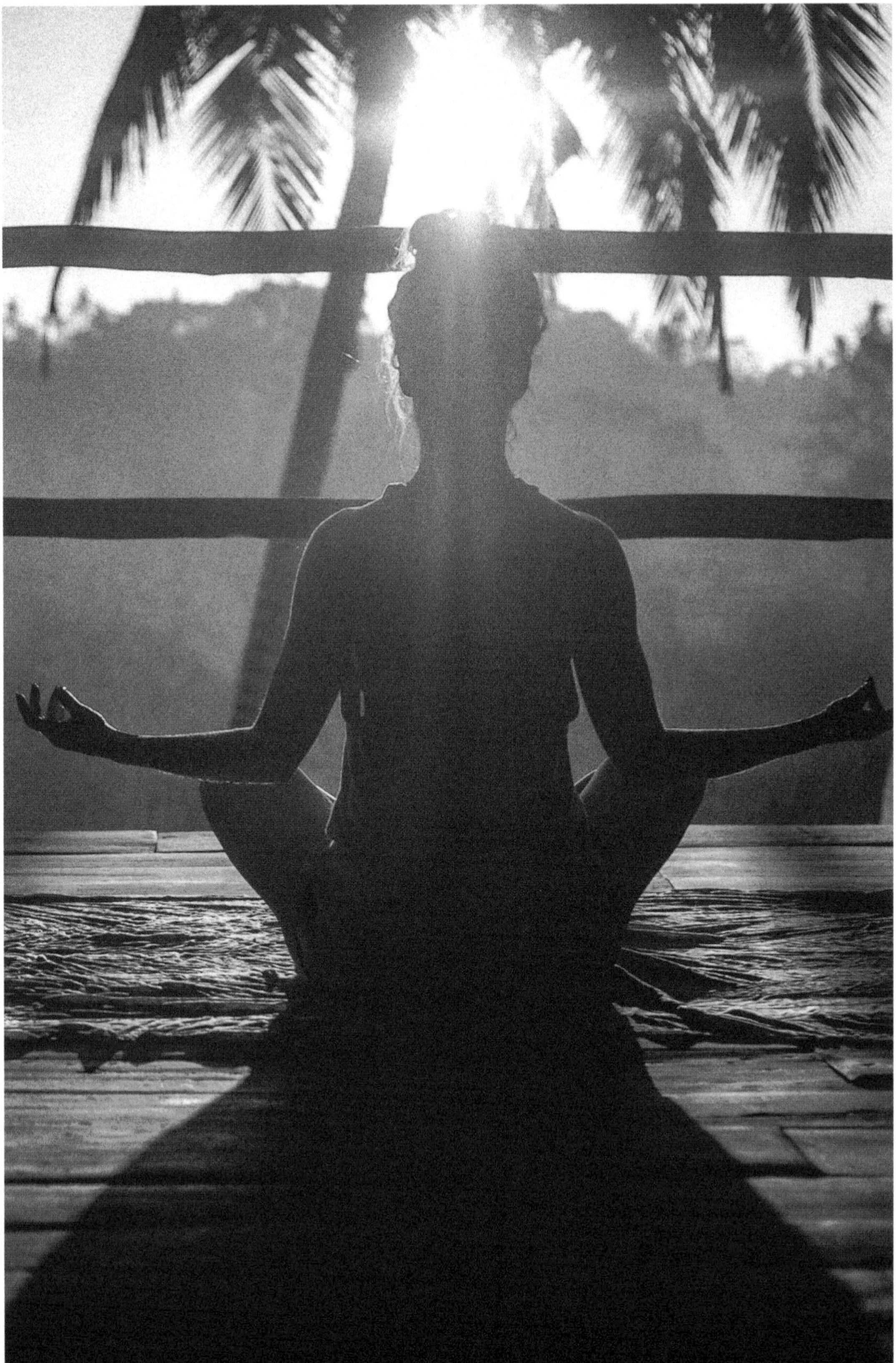

EXPLORE

Welcome to Month Four. You are doing so well already! In this chapter we will look at the importance of holistic health and wellness and what we can do to improve the relationship between body and mind.

Our body is our home for the duration of this life and a majestic miracle unparalleled by anything we will ever experience. We all tend to take our bodies for granted and with the easy availability of processed food, busy yet sedentary lives and a need for quick bursts of energy, it is far easier to make choices that affect our bodies adversely than it is to keep them clean and healthy. In fact, it can seem like an enormous battle to make healthy lifestyle choices, which for the most part are not supported by the world we live in.

Yet pain, sickness and any sort of deterioration of body and mind affects every single element of our lives, including the lives of those around us. But instead of looking into the future and giving up at the enormity and complexity of this one subject, we will approach it with the same calm level-headedness and step-by-step approach we have used for everything else.

Answer the following questions:

Overview

What score, out of five, did you give yourself for health and wellness in your Wheel of Life and why?

_____

_____

How is your health right now?

_____

_____

What are you tolerating at present?

_____

_____

What parts of your health and well-being are you happy with (diet, fitness etc.)?

_____

_____

What parts of your health and wellness do you feel you could work on?

_____

_____

Diet

Are you satisfied with your diet?

_____

_____

What areas of your diet could you improve?

_____

_____

Do you eat enough fruit and vegetables (5–10 portions per day)?

_____

_____

How could you introduce more healthy foods into your diet?

_____

_____

Exercise

How often do you exercise (daily/weekly/monthly)?

_____

_____

What are your favourite forms of exercise?

_____

_____

How could you incorporate more exercise into your weekly schedule?

_____

_____

Sleep

How many hours of sleep do you get on average every night?

_____

_____

What is your optimum number of hours sleep per night?

_____

_____

What time do you need to get to sleep at to achieve this?

_____

_____

What needs to happen for you to ensure you get this amount of sleep every night?

_____

_____

Conclusion

Which parts of your health and wellness need the most attention first?

_____

_____

What would need to happen for you to be able to focus on that?

_____

_____

EVERY NOW AND AGAIN,
YOU WILL FEEL A DULL ACHE
IN YOUR SOUL. A GENTLE
HUMMING AROUND YOUR
HEART. A LONGING FOR
SOMETHING WITHOUT A
NAME. IF I EVER TOLD YOU
TO OBEY ANYTHING, THIS
WOULD BE IT. LISTEN TO THE
CALL OF YOUR AUTHENTIC
SELF. THAT PART OF YOU
THAT LIVES JUST OUTSIDE
OF YOUR OWN SKIN. LET IT
HAVE ITS WAY WITH YOU.
I HAVE DIED A HUNDRED
TIMES TRYING TO IGNORE IT.

– Mia Hollow

MAKE YOUR MORNING MAGICAL

One of the greatest gifts I gave myself was the commitment to getting up early and carving out some time for myself in the morning. Right now, my life, like many other people's, is busy. While I am grateful for the responsibility that comes with raising children, it can feel like I'm swallowed up and disconnected to me. As the expression goes, the days are long but the years are short. I also noticed that the days I had to drag myself out of bed, crawling for the coffee in a bad mood, were the hardest. Nor were they great for anyone around me.

When I bit the bullet and started getting up early, despite the tiredness and the voice inside telling me to go back to sleep, I shifted a dynamic that in turn changed everything. I had a better start to the day and that helped me have a better day. Getting up early provided me with time to introduce some healthy practices in my life and that in turn started to reverse the cycle of tiredness, brain fog and general low energy I had been experiencing so often in the morning. I still love my morning coffee but the difference is this: I have it now because I *want* it, not because I *need* it.

If this is something that sounds appealing to you, here are some tips for getting up early.

Start realistically

Begin with getting up 30 minutes earlier to start. Ease your way in. If the time you set is too early, start again with a more realistic time. Increase this slowly.

Get up to something you enjoy

Choose something you love doing, rather than something you feel you 'should' be doing. A vigorous workout, stretch session or run might sound amazing to get in pre breakfast, yet if you have *any* resistance to exerting that amount of energy while the world sleeps it might hinder you actually doing it.

Even if you muscle through, manage on some mornings and feel great after, unless you fully enjoy the process, you won't make it any easier. Pick something that you really want to do, something you love. Breathing practice, meditation and relaxation are all great in the morning. Run a bath, read, write in your journal, prepare a healthy breakfast. Take a walk in nature, or go wild swimming. Watch the sunrise. Put the kettle on and make a hot drink that you enjoy. Making it easy and enjoyable will help you make that important shift from hearing the alarm clock to actually getting out of bed. And once you start your day this way, you are more likely to make time for intense physical activities later on.

Get to bed on time

It's pretty straightforward, but not getting enough sleep isn't going to help getting up early. Calculate how many hours of sleep you need and work back from there. Any extra is a bonus. If you need around 7.5 hours and wish to get up at 6.30 a.m., then make sure you're asleep by 11 p.m. ! The good news is the earlier you get up, the more tired you will be in the evening. I find that when I get into a cycle of later nights, school holidays for example, then I need to do a 'hard one', as I call it. A late night followed by an early morning. It's a little hard to begin with, but ensures I can get to bed at the right time that night, making the following morning easier. Hard ones don't happen often but it does work to break the cycle.

Consistency is key

Our body will adapt to the new time and it will start to get easier. Consistency is key. Even on lie-in days I am generally only adding an hour of sleep and waking naturally around the same time. Once you've made your decision to start, then keep it up! It will get easier.

Prepare the night before

Consider tidying up the night before so that when you get up, your living spaces are comfortable and clean. If you share a room with someone, think about having your clothes prepared so you don't have to turn on a light or make any noise and disturb them. These preparations are also intentions and will make the transition easier in the morning.

Don't give up

If at first you don't success, make it more realistic and try again. If you find you are snoozing for half the morning, or immediately turning the alarm off, you might have set goals too high. Pick a more realistic time to rise.

Let it go when it's time to let it go

Habit is great, but so is change and spontaneity. As is saying no. Listen to your body. Once a week or so I'll crawl back into bed again or not bother getting up at that early time. Finding balance has been key for me. I find I look forward to the following morning because I missed it when I didn't get up. It makes it easier. Sometimes it's good to say fuck it.

MOVE MORE

Our bodies are made for movement. Spend any amount of time in the company of children to realise that we move when we're happy and are happy when we're moving. Our sedentary lifestyle of desk-sitting and car-driving (and Netflix-bingeing) is a relatively recent addition to modern living and the knock-on effect is palpable in the deterioration of our collective health.

According to the World Health Organization (WHO), 60 to 85 per cent of the population worldwide does not engage in enough activity, making physical inactivity the fourth leading risk factor for global mortality. Now don't get me wrong, I don't wish to be transplanted back to a time of all-day toiling and back-breaking work – but there has to be a balance.

 ### Walking

I read a sobering thought in Bill Bryson's *A Walk in the Woods* where he endeavoured to hike the Appalachian Trail. He estimated that for every 20 minutes on the trail (carrying 20 kg's worth of tent, sleeping bag, stove, food and clothing) he was walking the same distance the average American walks *in a week*. A week! At first, I was shocked, then horrified, then judgemental. Once all that calmed down, I started looking at my own life and realised that perhaps I'm not too different to my cousins from across the pond. I began to investigate my own mileage in earnest. To my great surprise, I realised it wasn't exactly high. Living in the countryside as I do, many of the trips I make are by car: work, shops, school, kids' stuff. Unless I *go for a walk* then I'm not really walking. Don't get me wrong, I am incredibly busy and it can seem some days that I do not sit down from the moment I wake to the moment I crawl back into bed. Yet I wasn't making time to just walk.

Once I realised how little I was actually walking, I decided to do something about it – so I started to schedule walks. Scheduling walks may sound sterile and joyless, but making time in my life was an essential part of ensuring I got to do it.

One of the great benefits of doing this was that it got me back out into nature. Yes, my busy life as a working mother meant that I was clocking up my 10,000 steps per day easily enough, but the benefits I get from regular time outside, with a long stretch of road or trail ahead of me and nothing to do but put one foot in front of the other, has given me much more than mere mileage.

It has brought a calmness and a centre back into my life that resonates throughout my family. It is teaching me the impermanence of everything, from a hailstorm to the beautiful buds of spring. It is helping me to see the big picture more clearly. Getting out in hail, rain or shine blows off the cobwebs and resets my resolve. A walk tends to put everything into perspective and afterwards I sleep because I'm tired, eat because I'm hungry and sit down because I've just walked 10 km.

Walking is also a great opportunity to connect to another and a walk with a friend is a great way to spend time together. Being in nature, with someone we love, while moving our bodies and breathing fresh air is a tonic as well as a therapy. Our lives are busy and complicated and getting the chance to focus our attention on one person, a loved one, family member or friend is a true gift. Perhaps we might choose to walk with several different people or perhaps we will have one walking partner, but spending quality time with someone, the right person, literally feeds our soul and we get as much as we give.

Explore for more

Many wonderful things happen all the time right under our noses but unless we are actively seeking out these activities, they go unnoticed. Most communities organise charity races and hikes. Ireland is full of well-marked trails and looped walks and there are dozens of national parks with points of local interest that offer the opportunity to get out into nature and be active.

www.irishtrails.ie is a mine of information listing all the walking/hiking/cycling and kayaking ways in the country and lists them by county. There are many blogs and other information websites, not to mention YouTube channels, dedicated to sharing information on hiking and walking and once you start searching you will find so much going on all around you. Start with what you know and establish a positive habit first, then begin to explore and find new ways to keep up your interest.

Finding your own way

Perhaps you prefer running to walking or maybe getting out on your bike is your passion. Perhaps you like a mixture of all of it. It doesn't matter what gets you out into nature, just get out there and do it! Find someone who shares your interest and you're far more likely to stick to that commitment. Prioritise your continuing connection to nature and watch how it changes your life from the inside out.

'EAT FOOD, NOT TOO MUCH, MOSTLY PLANTS'

The whole nutrition issue can become confusing and overwhelming. There are so many diets – vegetarian, vegan, paleo, gluten-free, ketogenic, raw – and, frustratingly, these different approaches to food often work against one another. No wonder many of us stick our head in the sand and continue to eat as we have always done.

Essentially, what works for one person might not work for another. I have always looked for balance between what feels right and what is possible and after years of experimentation, personal research and the purchasing of *a lot* of books, I believe that I have finally landed on journalist Michael Pollan's simple philosophy: 'Eat food, not too much, mostly plants.' I LOVE this.

Years ago, my husband and I rented a large RV and took a road trip from San Francisco down Route 101 to LA. We collected the vehicle in Oakland and headed to the nearest supermarket to stock up on supplies. There was a large Walmart nearby, which happened to have ample parking for a vehicle our size. We had made a list of all that we needed and scurried around the massive store (there was even a McDonald's inside the shop) buying coffee, bread, the essentials. I couldn't find the fresh food section and eventually asked one of the shop assistants to point it out to me. As it turned out, the nice clerk informed me, they didn't have one.

Checking out, it dawned on me that this was a universal scene, one I was familiar with from my childhood. Tired parents, bored children – and still with the packing, unpacking and putting away to do – completing their weekly shop. Except that, in these trolleys, there was nothing that had grown in the ground, on a tree or in a bush. Perhaps these families went directly to their nearest organic produce suppliers to complete their shopping. Sadly, I suspect many did not.

Packets versus plants

When we walk into the supermarket and get past the fresh-produce section (assuming it has one, of course) we enter a whole new realm of culinary creations. The food in packets heralds a departure so great from what we have adapted to since the dawn of man that it is no wonder we are surrounded by so much disease. Yet, somewhere along the road, not only did food in a packet become the norm, but our lifestyles also changed so much that we now depend on its convenience.

We don't have to cook everything from scratch, but we can make an effort to eat more fresh food, more fruit, more vegetables. This is easy and manageable. A healthy diet gives us more energy, stabilises our weight, regulates our digestion, relieves brain fog, helps clear our skin, aids better sleep and generally helps us to feel well.

Eat when you're hungry

I'm a big advocate of only eating when I'm hungry. I've become used to tuning into my body's needs and not sticking rigidly to breakfast, lunch and dinner. This might sound unusual in this day and age, but it wasn't always so. The Romans didn't eat breakfast at all (despite having achieved quite a bit!) and the 'break-fast' meal did not become routine in the British Isles until the seventeenth century. During the Industrial Revolution breakfast became a part of the labourers' day simply because they needed a solid meal to sustain them for their early shifts down the mines.

Perhaps your work schedule requires you to stick to a format for eating that sustains you, but the next time you are off work and have a day to yourself, consider eating only when you are hungry. Also notice how much you eat: sticking to three square meals a day may mean we eat more than we need.

DRINK MORE WATER

We cannot survive without water. We know we should drink more. Yet for many of us, drinking water is a bore. No discernible flavour, an increased need for regular toilet visits … if we're not at any immediate risk, then why increase our water intake?

Staying well hydrated is giving our body the best chance to thrive, not merely survive.

Think of it this way. Like the light coming on in your car telling you the fuel tank is low, when the body feels thirst, you are already approaching dehydration. The difference in functioning on a full tank, so to speak, is extra energy, a smoother-functioning digestion, glowing skin and a clearer state of mind.

I ran a personal water experiment one summer when I was 18. I was working in a hotel and saving money to travel, so took every spare shift I could wrangle. Having both a tap and a toilet within feet of my workstation I started to knock back pint glasses of water at a ferocious rate. It took some time – my body needed to adjust. At first, my bladder struggled to keep up, but over the course of the summer my incredibly clever body adapted to the new regime and just like that, the constant need to go stopped.

What changed? From that day to this, over 23 years later, I continually receive compliments on my good skin and healthy glow. My energy levels soared and things just work better. My at-times sluggish digestion moves smoother, my immune system is strong. Maintaining a hydrated state has given me so many benefits that drinking a lot of water is just what I do now. It's who I am. It is not an effort. I know how much water I need, and I know long before thirst sets in when I am getting low.

The key is to start in the morning. Even before we break fast and eat our first meal, our body needs to hydrate. When we start the day with the huge advantages that staying well hydrated brings, we are already winning before we get dressed. So easy!

Hot or cold?

I lived in Hong Kong in my twenties where the summers were intolerably hot, with humidity of up to 95 per cent and temperatures of 30 degrees plus. My Chinese colleagues would look in horror as I gulped down litres of ice-cold water, never resisting the opportunity to tell me how unhealthy this was. This was news to me. So I did some research, and began to drink my water at room temperature. Then warm.

Even now in Ireland I am greeted with strange looks when I request a pint of warm water at the breakfast table in a hotel. It's just not in our culture. But our body temperature is 37 degrees Celsius, and filling our stomach with cold water, especially first thing in the morning, requires a lot of extra energy to cope with the temperature change – energy that could be put to better use waking us up, getting our digestive fluids flowing and preparing us for the day.

Supercharge your morning water

If life gives you lemons, drink them! Lemons contain so many useful nutrients, including vitamin C, as well as powerful antibacterial properties. Some of the benefits of adding lemons to your life include clearer skin, a boosted immune system, regulated PH plus other cold-fighting, anti-inflammatory, liver-cleansing, digestion-promoting, bowel-movement-regulating, detoxifying and infection-fighting benefits. Hard to believe when these little yellow orbs are so cheap and readily available in every corner shop.

Cut a lemon in half, use a fancy squeezer if you have one or just stick a teaspoon in the lemon half and turn as you squeeze it into your morning pint glass of warm water. Simple. Pips and bits will fall to the bottom of your glass. Make it quick and easy and you'll do it more often. If you don't like the taste of lemon in your water try adding a spoonful of honey or maple syrup. Do this for a few weeks and notice the change in your moods, your energy levels, your digestion and your skin.

What kind of water to drink

Tap water in Ireland is considered safe to drink yet our shops are stocked with bottles of drinking water. Bottled water is expensive and produces waste plastic but the choice between the two is hard for some people to make.

Sitting in the middle and a great option is to purchase a water filter. Under-the-sink water filters range in price and there is an option for every budget. Even for rental accommodation there are systems that require no hardwiring and the price per litre of filter water is far cheaper than bottled, and far cleaner, tastier and more chemical-free than tap. Options include reserve osmosis, ceramic filter and alkaliser systems. Each do different things: some simply filter out impurities while others filter chlorine and fluoride.

CREATE

Use your SMART goals to create a walking plan:

What five places could you walk in which are within an hour's travel from home?

_____

What days and times are you available to do this?

_____

_____

What equipment do you need (footwear, waterproofs, water bottles etc.)?

_____

_____

What is your start date for this plan?

_____

Commitment statement

Write a statement to yourself, committing to spend more time walking and more time in nature. Keep it realistic. Think about what you want and what will work for you.

Buy a reusable water bottle

Find a brand you like and think about the size you want. I always carry a one-litre bottle with me but some friends prefer 700 ml as it fits in their handbags. Spending some time on the purchase and finding a bottle you really like will mean you keep it close at all times. I have a range of bottles and keep them in my kitchen and car and it means I always have water on me and never need to buy bottled water.

Keep a food diary

Keeping a food diary of what we eat and how that correlates with how hungry we are is very useful. Our output might be higher some days than others; perhaps we cycled to work or went to a class or workout session before work. On those days we may be hungrier at lunchtime than normal. It makes sense to synchronise our food input to our energy output. If we are feeling low on energy, this might mean eating more to give us a boost, or eating less to keep our system feeling light. There is no right way or wrong way. When we begin to tune in to our body – *and our body is always talking to us* – becoming aware of the messages and signals it is sending ensures we will receive the information we need to sustain us in the best possible way.

MONTHLY REVIEW

Write down five things that you are inspired to try following this month.

1. _____

2. _____

3. _____

4. _____

5. _____

MY NOTES

MY NOTES

MY NOTES

MY NOTES

MY NOTES

MY NOTES

MONTH FIVE
Stress and Relaxation

YOU ONLY LIVE ONCE, BUT IF YOU DO IT RIGHT, ONCE IS ENOUGH.

– *Mae West*

EXPLORE

Welcome to Month Five. I hope that you are starting to notice the effects of this journey rippling out into all the areas of your life and that your sense of purpose and state of mind are strong and positive. The theme for this month is one I am especially passionate about and committing to it myself has been something I have focused on a lot in the last few years, especially with the work I do at my retreat.

Stress plays a huge factor in our health and is the scourge of our busy lives. In this chapter we will discuss stress and ways to overcome it. I will share some ideas here that will hopefully help you if this is something important you want to focus on.

How stressed do you feel at this time in your life?

_____

_____

What are the stressors in your life?

_____

_____

What are your coping strategies for stress?

_____

_____

How do you feel stress impacts your life? Think in terms of physical and mental health.

_____

_____

How much time per week do you devote to your own health, happiness and well-being?

_____

_____

What are your favourite self-care routines?

_____

_____

How important is rest and recovery to you?

_____

_____

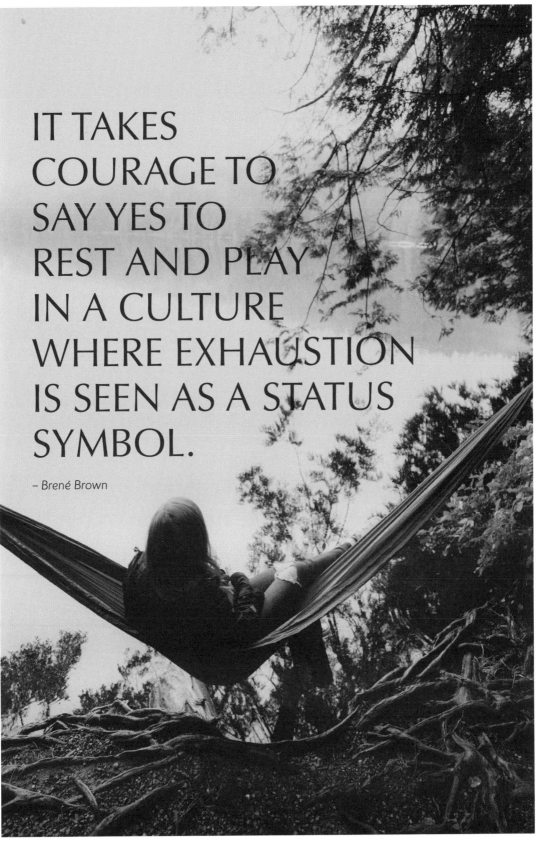

IT TAKES
COURAGE TO
SAY YES TO
REST AND PLAY
IN A CULTURE
WHERE EXHAUSTION
IS SEEN AS A STATUS
SYMBOL.

– Brené Brown

Rest and relaxation

We live in a world where we've been told we have to work hard to achieve what we deserve. We have grown up being told by society that things aren't right the way that they are, and that we have to change them to make them the way they should be. Very few of us would admit that we completely love and adore all parts of our body, yet our miracle body is without doubt the greatest gift we will ever receive.

More and more people are struggling with sleep disorders, chronic diseases and mental health issues, yet it doesn't seem our lifestyles support the type of rest and recovery that is needed to survive this modern life.

Professional athletes have built-in recovery time that is a part of their paid jobs. If they don't recover, they can't perform. I believe it's the same in all walks of life. Not only can we not perform, we cannot heal.

Healing

The body and mind are constantly helping to bring us back to equilibrium. Our immune system is always working on our behalf. We cut our finger – it will heal. We develop a cold – we recover. When we are sick, we know we need to rest. It is through rest that our body can begin the healing process.

We need this rest all the time and not just when we are sick. I'm not talking about the sort of rest that involves lying on the couch and watching telly, but the type of deep relaxation that changes the brainwave frequency and begins a whole set of healing processes. We can drink another coffee and get some energy that way, but to really start to create pure energy on a cellular level, we need to recharge properly.

OUR BODY AND MIND ARE CONNECTED. WHEN WE RELAX THE BODY IT RELAXES THE MIND, AND WHEN WE RELAX THE MIND IT RELAXES THE BODY.

A little goes a long way. Even ten minutes of proper relaxation can make a big difference. Real rest means no distractions, no phones, no reading, no chatting. No strong physical sensations (deep stretches), just simple, pleasurable rest.

Finding stillness

Finding stillness is an essential way of maintaining our health. Once we get into a habit of rest, we can start to bring it into our lives in more ways.

I've worked as a yoga teacher since 2004, and as I have primarily taught on retreats I have seen the benefits of rest and relaxation with my own eyes. I have developed my own style of slow, restorative and yin yoga practices that are generally done over two hours during an evening class.

Over this time, I have witnessed the remarkable change in people from slowing down and resting. It's uncanny. I see the change in their faces, I hear it in the way they speak and I sense it being in their company. Getting off the metaphorical treadmill – actually stopping, and stepping off – can have a profound effect on every aspect of our lives.

One of our greatest assets as humans is our ability to adapt. When life gets busy we become so used to that state that we don't know what to do when things calm down And so we maintain the busyness – we find things to do when we don't *actually* need to do anything. With those handy little devices we carry around with us everywhere we go, there is no shortage of distraction. We rely on being distracted as it's all we know. Busy becomes our habit, a pattern that we practise so much it becomes who we are.

But it is not who we are. Changing our habits is part of the solution, but it isn't the only one. We must undo the damage done to the adrenal glands, to the body, to the mind and to the whole self to relearn our natural state. We also have to forgive ourselves. This is a part of the process.

Rest and digest

It all comes back to the nervous system. Think of us as prehistoric man. Outside the cave we are in danger of attack and so our body responds by putting into effect a chain of actions to deflect this. Our pupils dilate so we can take in more visual information. The liver creates more insulin to give us more energy. The heart pumps faster to circulate more blood around the body. Our digestion adapts: we no longer feel hunger, allowing us to have more energy for action. Our breathing pattern changes. Our immune system creates inflammation to protect our body from viruses, pathogens and bacteria in this vulnerable state. In short, our body functions a lot differently when we are outside the cave than it does when we are inside it. If we are being chased by a bear, how much of our potential energy do we need? All of it of course! And so, our body adapts to give us 100 per cent of the possible energy it can generate in this life-threatening situation. But this state cannot be sustained for long periods: it's extremely taxing on the body and it is essential that it is recovered from afterwards.

Recovery

Inside the cave is where we heal. Not just emotionally, but actual physical healing. We sleep. Rest. Eat. Recover. Digestion begins again, hunger comes upon us and we assimilate the nutrients from the food we have hunted and gathered. Our heart rate slows down. Our blood pressure drops. Our breathing calms. We are in recovery mode. We need this. The busier our 'outside' life, the more stressful our daily situation and the more we need 'cave' rest. There is no shortcut, no diet, no pill and no physical exercise that can recover the body from stress in the same way.

WE NEED TO REST TO RECOVER.

OUTSIDE CAVE		INSIDE CAVE
Dilated, taking in more info	EYES	Contracted, relaxed state
No saliva, digestion stops	MOUTH	Saliva present, digestion starts
Inflammation created to protect	IMMUNE	Healing of injury/illness
Beats faster, more blood	HEART	Slows down, relaxes
Breathing faster, more O$_2$	LUNGS	Slow down, relax
More insulin, more energy	LIVER	Slows down insulin production
Peristalsis and digestion stops	DIGESTION	Peristalsis and digestion resumes

Outside the cave, inside the cave

One of the biggest issues we face in the modern world is how plugged in we are. We are online, available and ready for action *all the time*. In other words, we are *outside* the cave when we are *inside* the cave. This is not good for the nervous system. Our body was not made to sustain the physical characteristics of stress for any prolonged length of time. Our body was built for stress, yes, but it is only hardwired to sustain stress for short bursts of time and then to recover from it.

Stress itself isn't the problem. The stress response is a healthy and natural reaction of the body that is life-saving and vital for survival. Stress, and the release of the hormones noradrenaline and cortisol, is what saves us in emergency situations and helps us find that extra energy to escape from a dangerous situation.

Here is where it gets interesting: the body doesn't know the difference between *physical* stress and *mental* stress, or between a bear about to attack and an email containing disturbing news. The reaction is the same and activates the sympathetic nervous system: our outside-the-cave response. But when the bear runs back into the woods and the stressful situation is over, our body recovers. Yet for many of us, our lives are so busy, connected and full of stressful situations *all the time* that our body doesn't recover. And that's the big problem.

Stress isn't the problem. Not recovering from stress is the problem.

ONE SMALL CHANGE

Making changes towards a healthier lifestyle can feel overwhelming. Using our innate wisdom to filter the many choices out there is a critical part of the process, but we cannot do this in survival mode, which is tiring and taxing. It might seem like a chicken-and-egg scenario, but through proper relaxation, we can begin to heal the parts of ourselves that need to be healed. We can start to bring the body back to balance. We can release tension from the mind. And we can begin to make decisions for ourselves from the seat of compassion and respect that will know intimately what is right for us.

WHAT IS THE RELATIONSHIP BETWEEN STRESS, RELAXATION AND WEIGHT?

This is a controversial topic as there are many factors that can determine our relationship to gaining and losing weight. Genetics plays a large part, as does lifestyle, profession, family and community, location, access to food, socio-demographics and each person's unique physical make up and medical history.

This section is not intended to suggest that losing weight is easy or attainable by relaxation alone, but it is generally accepted that *eating better and moving more* are the two keys to weight loss.

I propose a third key that is vital to success – breathing.

STRESS IS NOT CAUSED BY A SITUATION. IT IS CAUSED BY HOW WE REACT TO THAT SITUATION.

The magic porridge pot

If life is continually stressful, or at least our reaction to it, then the body goes into continual cortisol and noradrenalin production. The longer we are in a state of stress the more the body learns that these hormones are constantly needed. The overproduction of these hormones places strain on the adrenal glands (where they are secreted), which wreaks havoc on many of our other bodily functions and can cause fatigue and depression. But worse still is that the body 'forgets' how to switch it off. It's like the magic porridge pot: it keeps producing these hormones and it becomes self-perpetuating. And one area that is greatly affected by the over-production of these hormones, cortisol in particular, is weight control.

Rewiring

This might all sound quite depressing, but there is a simple and effective way to overcome this. We relearn – or rewire – how to turn off stress and so better manage our reactions to situations. Depending on the individual, the level of stress and length of time in stress, this can take any amount of time. But one thing is for sure, even the shortest relaxation can have the most profound effect. I know this from experience.

THE BREATH

At the beginning there was the breath. It is the first thing we do when we come into this world and the last thing we do when we leave. It is our life force and it is our connection to the divine. Oxygen is our most essential nutrient and our breath is the bridge between our body and our mind.

Our breathing determines our state of mind, the PH levels in our blood and the chemistry in our cells. But because it is an automatic response of the body, (we do not *choose* to breathe), many of us don't give it too much thought. However, we can modify *how* we breathe. And how we breathe affects our entire state of being.

Breathing plays a huge part in our body's basic functioning, and if it isn't done optimally then our body will not function optimally. A chemical reaction happens in our cells between stored energy from the food we eat and the oxygen we breathe. This chemical reaction creates ATP (adenosine triphosphate), which is what gives us energy for physiological processes such as muscle contractions. It happens deep in the mitochondria of the cells, in every cell in our body. If this reaction doesn't occur optimally because of poor breathing and insufficient oxygen, the stored energy isn't burned for fuel/energy and remains in the body.

The nervous system and our breath

How we breathe affects how we feel. And learning how to use our breathing properly is the single most effective way to control stress. Think of your nervous system as divided into two parts: sympathetic and para-sympathetic or, in simple terms, fight or flight and rest and digest.

Let's return to the cave analogy. The interesting and important aspect of this model is that all the organs function autonomically, except one: our lungs and our breath.

And here's the third key I mentioned earlier: by manually changing our breathing we can stop stress. Changing our breath, from rapid and shallow to slow and deep, changes our nervous system from stressed to relaxed.

By learning and practising new breathing techniques, we can choose to move into a rest-and-digest state, in which the body will naturally begin the healing process.

Our body wants to heal itself: we can watch a scab forming on a cut or feel a bone knit back together in a cast to know that. But it cannot heal when it is in fight-or-flight mode.

The price for remaining for long periods in this survival mode is detrimental on our body and our mind. Burnout, insomnia, inflammatory conditions including depression, and a long list of chronic diseases are some of the symptoms of being in a constant state of stress. However, taking the time every day to breathe deeply and properly can totally and utterly reverse this.

We can control the state of our mind and thus control the state of our body. And it is something that we can do for free, anytime, anywhere. It is empowering and, most importantly, it works.

 ### The vagus nerve

The vagus nerve travels from the back of the neck down through the entire nervous system. It plays a major role in regulating our heart rate and carries information from our internal organs back to the brain. When we breathe deeply, we stimulate the vagus nerve, which is in charge of turning our fight-or-flight reflex on and off. This in turn activates our relaxation response, reducing our heart rate and blood pressure. Breathing slowly and deeply allows us to change our nervous system from fight or flight to rest and digest.

We feel better. We are no longer feeling the stress. We are in charge again.

TRY IT YOURSELF:
TAKE TEN LONG DEEP YOGIC BREATHS

1. Lie on your back and place your hands on your tummy.

2. As you inhale, feel your tummy rise. As you exhale, feel it drop.

3. Focus on your exhale.

4. Keep exhaling and when you think you cannot exhale any further, try to: the next inhale will be fuller and deeper.

5. Begin to fill your chest on the next inhale, sending the air out laterally into the side ribs.

6. Exhale completely, even contracting the belly slightly to exhale further.

7. As you inhale, imagine you are filling three separate containers:

    *   Your belly

    *   Your ribs

    *   Your upper chest

8. Lengthen each exhale. Count ten breaths like this, lengthening each one.

9. A count that might work for you is: inhale for four, exhale for eight.

10. Once this is comfortable you can begin to lengthen it: inhale for five, exhale for ten. And so on.

11. When you finish, allow your breathing to return to normal. Notice how you feel.

YOGA

Yoga is a natural option for many people searching for relaxation. Even in a physical class where the body is challenged, people find great release by moving the body before settling down for a nice relaxation at the end. Most classes are 1 – 1.5 hours long yet it's common for savasana (the relaxation part at the end) to be less than five minutes long. It seems that even yoga has become caught up in a list of to-do's and goals where relaxation gets overlooked!

Restorative, slow and yin-based yoga, somatic movement

As a natural balance to this, there are other forms of yoga and movement where the primary focus is relaxation and these forms of yoga are growing in popularity. Running a retreat centre myself where every evening we do a two-hour yoga class focused on relaxation, I find it interesting that people often feel it is decadent to spend two hours doing very little (or so it seems!). To me it feels wrong that we treat slowing down and recharging as a luxury. I actually see it as survival.

When our smartphones are running low on battery we do what we can to plug them in before they run out entirely. We know that charging them from completely dead takes much longer. We *need* to do this for our bodies and minds, but still the general perception is that a restorative yoga class is a luxury. I hope this changes soon.

MEDITATION

Meditation has long been known for changing the brain wave frequencies and promoting relaxation. A seated meditation can be paired with a lying-down relaxation. Meditation helps us to release the control of our thoughts on our experience, which allows us to come out of the mind and into the body. A successful meditation practice is challenging for many people but the rewards are enormous and a lot of research and studies have proven their effectiveness in conquering stress.

Guided relaxation and yoga nidra

While moving the body is a great way to achieve a greater state of relaxation, at the end of the day simply practising relaxation will get us there too. This works well if we are in a hurry, as taking time out for a yoga class may affect the frequency with which we practise relaxation. I am a big fan of guided relaxations and simply lying down or getting comfortable and listening to them. There are so many great apps available, including relaxations to recharge and to prepare for sleep. Many of these adopt a self-hypnosis model.

Yoga nidra (pronounced 'nee-dra') is an ancient practice said to be as old as time itself. Emanating from India, the first recordings date back to 1000 BCT. It is a practice that brings us into that space between sleep and wakefulness, where deep healing on all levels of our being can occur. There has been a resurgence in modern times as people recognise the strong need for deep relaxation. Yoga nidra is more than the ten minutes' rest at the end of a yoga class; it is its own practice and can be done in conjunction with a class, or as a stand-alone experience.

Ultimately, in order to become good at anything we need to practise, and little and often is best. Five minutes a day is better than 30 minutes once a week. Our brains will learn and our body will follow, so while all the suggestions above are useful, if you really want to retrain the body to relax then my personal favourite is to do as many guided relaxation sessions as you can. Getting to a slow or restorative yoga class is an added bonus. In the beginning it may be hard – in fact savasana (final relaxation pose) is often referred to as the hardest pose of all.

Relaxation is a gift that will keep unfolding and it is a practice that deserves a firm place in any wellness-seeker's weekly routine.

CREATE

Write a list of five activities that you find deeply relaxing (taking a bath, painting etc.).

1. _____

2. _____

3. _____

4. _____

5. _____

MAKE TIME IN YOUR WEEK FOR ONE 20-MINUTE RELAXATION PER WEEK:

1. Lie down.

2. Get comfortable.

3. Set the scene – candles, lighting etc.

4. Set a timer (but turn your phone off!).

5. Play some relaxing music if that's helpful.

6. Start with ten deep yogic breaths.

7. Play a recorded relaxation or simply stick with the music.

Journal about your experience each week. Notice how this is affecting your mood, your day, your sleep. Chart your progress. Stick with it and watch how this simple practice starts to change your life from the inside out.

MONTHLY REVIEW

What was your take-home from this month?

_____

_____

_____

_____

_____

What have you learned about stress?

_____

_____

_____

_____

_____

How can you better integrate relaxation into your life?

_____

_____

_____

_____

_____

MY NOTES

MY NOTES

MY NOTES

MY NOTES

MY NOTES

MY NOTES

MONTH SIX
Reflecting and Moving Forward

THE GREATER DANGER FOR MOST OF US LIES NOT IN SETTING OUR AIM TOO HIGH AND FALLING SHORT, BUT IN SETTING OUR AIM TOO LOW AND ACHIEVING OUR MARK.

– Michelangelo

EXPLORE

We are almost halfway through the book now so well done for
sticking with it. In this chapter we will review our journey to date
and consider again what it is we want and where we want to go.

List three wonderful changes that you have brought into your life since the beginning of this book.

1. _____

2. _____

3. _____

List three goals you would like to achieve in the next three months.

1. _____

2. _____

3. _____

Revisit your Wheel of Life from Month One (p. 15) and compare it to when you first started the journey.

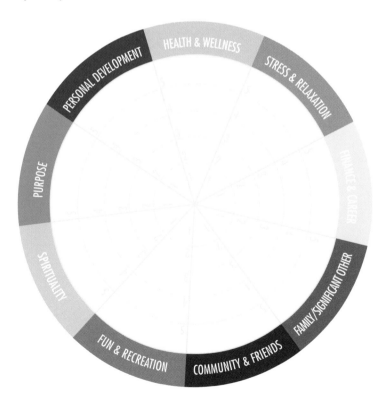

List three areas of your wheel on which you have made some improvements.

1. _____

2. _____

3. _____

List three areas of your wheel that you would like to focus more on in the following months.

1. _____

2. _____

3. _____

Check in

How is your journal writing going?

_____

_____

Has it been helpful?

_____

_____

If you have discontinued writing, would you consider starting it up again?

_____

_____

Digital detox

One of the biggest distractions that constantly gets in the way of doing, being and living our best lives is spending too much time online. As a mother I'm acutely aware of not letting my kids spend too much time on screens. Like many parents, the worry of how this will affect their development is ever present. It was a wake-up call for me the day I realised that it wasn't their screen time I needed to be aware of, but my own. Monkey see, monkey do and all that, but it's how this affects me that is my biggest concern. This applies to all of us, parents or not.

The sobering fact of the matter is this: when weighing up the pros and cons, the benefits and the negatives, the conclusion is that too much screen time has a very negative effect on our lives. From contributing to mental illness to causing dissatisfaction when comparing our lives to our perception of others' lives. From addiction and lack of control to online bullying and encouraging low self-esteem with fake or false realities.

But most of all, the sobering fact of just how many hours of our one precious life we waste staring into a small plastic box is by far the worst. Time we could be spending in connection with people. Time we could be spending in connection with nature. Time we could be spending in connection with ourselves.

THE REAL QUESTION WE NEED TO ASK OURSELVES IS THIS: IS OUR ONLINE EXPERIENCE ENHANCING OUR LIFE OR HARMING IT?

The man who invented the continuing or 'infinite' scroll (the never-ending feed on our social media platforms showcasing the lives of the people we follow), Aza Raskin, has confessed that he regrets it now, seeing how it has changed the fabric of all our lives. 'Behind every screen on your phone, there are […] literally a thousand engineers that have worked on this thing to try to make it maximally addicting,' he said. 'If you don't give your brain time to catch up with your impulses,' Mr Raskin added, 'you just keep scrolling.'

There are private treatment facilities cropping up all over the world where addiction to devices, gaming and being online is being addressed in the same way as alcohol and drug disorders. We are becoming increasingly addicted to our screens and the treatment is extremely expensive and out of reach for most people.

Who's in control?

There are many advantages to online applications and resources, but when they are in control of us and not the other way around, we are in trouble. Here are a few questions you can ask yourself to determine if a digital detox might be a necessary step for you.

1. Do you reach for your phone habitually?

2. Is looking at your phone the first thing you do in the morning?

3. Is looking at your phone the last thing you do at night?

4. Do you find yourself looking at your phone when you are alone?

5. If you are sitting in a café or a restaurant with your friend and they leave to visit the bathroom or get a coffee, do you find yourself automatically reaching for your phone?

6. When experiencing something unique, beautiful or adventurous, is your first thought to share it on social media?

7. You take a stunning photo – is your first thought to share it on social media?

8. Do you have your phone on you at all times?

If you have answered yes to any of these questions, perhaps you need a digital detox. Here are a few suggestions to get you started.

Make airplane mode your best friend. Get used to putting your phone on silent.

It might sound simple, but here is the truth. Unless you're a doctor on call, you don't need to be available *all the time*. Especially when we are not at work. We managed without this disturbance for millennia and we can relearn it. It won't take long before we get used to not having our phone on us or turned on all the time. We do not have to get back to people immediately. We most certainly do not need to break a real face-to-face conversation to look at something on our phone, whether that is a message or a notification. Like any addiction, if it is in control of us, we are in trouble. With the caveat of needing it for safety, turning our phone on silent or leaving it behind occasionally is a powerful step towards taking back control.

Turn off notifications from your favourite apps.

This is a simple step, but means app-action stays within apps. When the notifications pop up on the phone, we might be drawn in with less time to think about whether we actually want to be on our phone at that time or not.

Leave groups in which you are not active.

As well as being unhealthy and nosy, it is incredibly time-wasting to lurk in a group you're not part of. Send a text to say you are making an effort to be off your device and so are leaving groups you are not active in. You'll be setting a good example.

Limit personal social media use to designated times.

This is something parents often do with young kids. Many of us do not allow our smallies to have free rein over TV, games and other online apps and use methods of timing and scheduling for when they do. Consider adopting some of those practices on yourself. Allow yourself a half an hour in the evening (or better still three evenings a week) to indulge guilt-free. Consider charting your app use with the many new features that allow you to do this. Cut it down!

Get back into books or get into them.

The writing is on the wall: reading a book is far more life-enhancing, healthy, inspiring and generally better for you than any amount of online action. Join your local library, visit a second-hand bookstore, or support your local bookshop. Find a book that hooks you instantly. Immerse yourself in it and then get another. And another. Books allow us to enter into a creative state in our brain, which leaves us with a feeling of well-being. Does spending time on social media *always* leave you feeling good?

Probably not. Screens, and the blue light that emanates from them, mess with our circadian rhythm and interferes with our sleep. Books do not. The joy of a great book, a story that penetrates deep into our consciousness and stays with us forever is indeed a great gift. Endless social-media scrolling cannot stand up to this.

Set a cut-off time before bed and a cut-off time to turn on again in the morning.

Turn your phone to airplane mode at night and decide how many hours before and after sleep you will keep it this way. In the mornings, I do not turn my phone on until 20 minutes before I leave the house. Mornings are my sacred time and leaving it on airplane mode means I will not be disturbed. Mornings can be a time for positive habits, setting the scene for the whole day and finding a little 'me time' in an otherwise full day. Leave the phone out of it. Likewise at night-time, the chance to unwind, review and let go of the day is best done with full presence of mind and no distractions.

Observe your use. Notice when you reach for your phone and begin to resist the pull.

The first step to changing something is to become aware of it. Many of us are in denial as to how attached we are to our phones, never mind whether we may have an addiction. Start to become aware of your own use. Catch yourself as you reach for your phone to browse. Can you stop yourself? When you go to your phone to make a call or send a text, do you end up browsing then too? Do you find yourself suddenly lost in you app, wondering how you got there and what your original purpose was when you opened your phone?

Try to stop yourself. Take a few deep breaths and let the impulse wash over you and pass. Start to become aware of your phone usage in a conscious and mindful way. This will teach you a lot about your habit.

Family time

If you have kids, consider setting a rule that you do not browse in front of them – save it for when they are asleep or during your designated times. Making phone calls and texts is different and a whole other topic, but leave the scrolling for when you are not being so closely observed.

MOVING ON

Now that you've had a chance to think about how far you have come, it is time to put that behind you and move on. The important thing is to acknowledge your effort to make any amount of time to focus on yourself, whether it has been successful or not. By even contemplating this journey you are showing up for yourself in the most powerful way. That is what is significant. We can let go of the quality of what we have done – we must, in fact, not be attached to any perceived outcome of our work. Any time we spend on our goals, our dreams and our healing is important. It is not our job, now, to look back at what we did or did not do, but to focus on all that we can and have yet to do.

As we move into the second part of the year, we will move in the direction of love, relationships, finances and how we show up in this life. Well done for staying on the path, you are doing a great job. Know that.

IT CANNOT
BE SAID TOO
OFTEN; ALL LIFE
IS ONE. THAT IS,
AND I SUSPECT
WILL FOREVER
PROVE TO BE,
THE MOST
PROFOUND
TRUE
STATEMENT
THERE IS.

– Bill Bryson

HOW TO GET SHIT DONE!

Why is it that so many of us struggle to do the very things we know deep down we need to do? It's simple. We allow ourselves to be ruled by our mind. Perhaps it's fear, or a deep-rooted disbelief in ourselves, but either way, the more we *want* something, the more we *know* something is beneficial to us, the more our minds resist it.

But here's the key: that resistance is easy to overcome. Just as the mind can trick us, we can just as easily train it. And like training a dog, it takes patience, dedication and small consistent steps.

One of the ways the mind fools us is when we get bogged down with our goals. We set ourselves unrealistic tasks, which actually set us up to fail before we even begin! Does this sound familiar?

Another way the mind fools us is the future clause: When I have moved into that new place then I will … When I'm back from that trip I will start … When I've finished that project, I can begin …

The mind has won before we got out of the starting gate.

So how do we get shit done? The answer is slowly, bit by bit.

Start by looking at what you want in life. What would make you happier right now? Is it yoga home practice? Is it eating healthier? Keep the goal as what it is: a goal, a destination, and final point, but change the route. For example, if mornings are not working for you then find another time.

Make it easy. That 60-minute home practice, start with 20 minutes. Make a chart, copy some cells online or draw it with your hand. Have it available to see and set REALISTIC steps towards your goal. Look at it, then make it even more realistic. Maybe 10 minutes. Make a rule: never miss twice in a row (unless in extreme circumstances). Mark each day off with a flourish. It won't take long. Between 30 and 90 days is popularly believed to be the length it takes to form a new habit.

Even making plans about how to achieve our goals is another trick of the mind to delay working towards them so keeping the initial steps simple and realistic is helpful here too.

One thing at a time. Here's another one to watch out for. We can get carried away and think we can take on the world. But the reality is that the world will keep turning and another year will pass and we won't have achieved even one of those things. So just pick one. Maybe you want to work on handstands. Well focus on this, and this alone. Spend five minutes a day doing this, each day, every day. Mark it off as you go along and before you know it you WILL have achieved your goal. Or writing, or eating better – it doesn't matter. The process is the same.

It is simple. And yet, this simplicity eludes us, another trick of the mind.

You see, the mind really is its own worst enemy because it doesn't know what it's missing. It doesn't know what's good for it, because it's always things we haven't yet mastered that it is resisting. So, bit by bit, the more we do our 'thing', the mind will learn it doesn't have anything to fear, that it won't be threatened by change and life in fact, will become sweeter.

The truth is simple. Stop complicating it and start getting it done. Life moves fast and before you know it you will have started to master yourself with one goal successfully achieved. Then another and another and so on. Start today, this exact minute in fact. No more excuses.

To recap

1. Recognise that your mind will find a way to resist what is really important to you. Send love to your mind and do it anyway.

2. Let go of the big ideas and start really small and simple.

3. Start right now and don't allow that mind to make excuses, it's what it does!

CREATE

Refer back to the beginning of this chapter and find the answers to the following question.

List three goals you would like to achieve in the next three months.

1. _____

2. _____

3. _____

For each goal, you can break it down into five bite-sized pieces (SMART goals) in your journal.

For example:

Goal: I want to lose 2 lbs

Bite-sized pieces:

1.   Walk three times a week.

2.   Switch to green smoothies for breakfast.

3.   Attend two HIIT classes at the gym per week.

Write out three ways you can minimise your online usage. Create three new instructions for yourself. For example, turn my phone onto airplane mode at 9 p.m. at night and do not turn it back on until 9 a.m. in the morning.

Rule 1

_____

Rule 2

_____

Rule 3

_____

MONTHLY REVIEW

What was your biggest take-home from this chapter?

Are you noticing any changes in your life as a result of this work?

Write a paragraph of praise to yourself from the perspective of 'future you' for the efforts you have made so far in prioritising your wellness, body, mind and soul. Use positive, kind and encouraging words. Don't take this bit too seriously; have fun with it. Imagine you are a teacher writing a school report to a top student to encourage them for the year ahead.

_____

_____

_____

_____

_____

_____

_____

_____

_____

What areas of your life would you most like to focus on for the remainder of this year? List three areas in order of importance, for example: health, career, social life.

1. _____

2. _____

3. _____

MY NOTES

MY NOTES

MY NOTES

MY NOTES

MY NOTES

MY NOTES

MONTH SEVEN
Thriving – Finance and Career

ACKNOWLEDGING
THE GOOD THAT
YOU ALREADY
HAVE IN YOUR
LIFE IS THE
FOUNDATION FOR
ALL ABUNDANCE.

– *Eckhart Tolle*

EXPLORE

Welcome to Month Seven, where we delve into the muddy waters of money and career. Money is a particularly emotional topic and in short supply for many of us. Our opinions and feelings around money, like everything else, can stem from our childhood experiences and for a lot of us it can feel like an area of our life that is controlling us and not the other way around.

Taking stock

Everyone's needs are different when it comes to our work satisfaction and financial security. Our lifestyles all vary and our demographic, location and responsibilities contribute to our living costs and our expenditure. We might live in a city where we have a big mortgage but a high-paying job, or we might live in the countryside where employment options are fewer but living costs are lower. What is important is that we are living comfortably within our means and that we are not feeling stressed around our finances.

Whether we work full-time taking care of our home (which is a lot more than 37.5 hours per week, incidentally), have a part-time or full-time job, are self-employed or anything in between, if we don't feel satisfied, valued or appreciated and are constantly stressed about money, then it might be time to address our connection with money face on.

Financial well-being

Financial well-being is a large section on most major banks' websites and something that Irish people score very low on compared to our European neighbours.

My bank has a short online quiz where you answer eight questions with multiple-choice answers regarding bill-paying, debt, savings, insurance and so on. You are awarded a score out of 100 per cent depending on how you are managing, and the bank offers a service where any issues can be explored further so that a plan can be made to bring up the score.

Financial well-being addresses the underlying issue of financial stress by facing our situation directly and seeing how manageable it is. Instead of burying our heads in an ever-growing mountain of bills, we meet it head on and start to work our way through, step by step. It's well worth asking your bank to see what financial well-being services they offer in order to find out how you are faring in this area.

Balancing what we do and what we earn is challenging for many of us as, depending on our responsibilities and debt, our choices may appear limited. Job satisfaction may appear higher or lower on the importance scale depending on one's particular situation and it is certainly not a one-size-fits-all model.

THINK ABOUT THE FOLLOWING QUESTIONS:

What would I do if I had more money?

_____

_____

What material things do I need?

_____

_____

Do I want a more fulfilling career or business?

_____

_____

If I won the lottery would I give up my job?

_____

_____

What messages about money did I hear growing up?

_____

_____

On a scale of 1–10, how motivated are you in your professional life right now? What is it that motivates you?

_____

_____

On a scale of 1 – 10, how satisfied are you with your current financial situation?

_____

_____

What do you have to bring to the world?

_____

_____

If anything was possible, what would you wish for?

_____

_____

If you could manifest anything for your life right now, what would it be?

_____

_____

If you had to leave the house all day, every day, where would you go and what would you do?

_____

_____

How are you going to make a difference to the world?

_____

_____

CONTEMPLATE

Finances

Money is a funny one, and I mean funny peculiar. In essence, it is just energy exchange. Something we exchange for something else. Housing, services and products have a price, and when the barter system no longer suited the masses, a way of measuring and matching the value of that exchange became necessary: money was born.

People, too, are funny around money. It is the reason behind the collapse of civilizations, the root of war and famine, and is still the cause of many relationship break-ups. We don't only deal with money in reference to how much we have or don't have; when we open a conversation about money, we are also dealing with our past, the current political environment and our community. Money and the many emotions it stirs runs deep, yet on the surface it is not a subject many of us are comfortable with.

It is worth taking the time to think about our relationship with money, because if we think of money for what it is – an exchange – we might find that 'money' is a lot more about who we are, where we came from and our core beliefs than the pieces of paper that represent it. Once we have a clear view of how our history might be shaping our relationship with money, we can see that it is not a set standard and we can begin to examine this relationship and make changes where needed. If we are holding on to painful memories around money from childhood, unless we consciously examine this and choose to move past it, our connection with money will always be marred. Later in this chapter we will explore tools that can help us with our financial goals, but for now let's look a little deeper into our relationship with money.

What is your history with money? Consider the following questions and write down your answers.

Did you receive pocket money when you were young? What did you do with it?

_____

_____

Did you have a bank account when you were a child? What did you do with your savings?

_____

_____

Was money plentiful or scarce when you were growing up?

_____

_____

When did you get your first job? What was it and what did you do with the money you earned?

_____

_____

Do you have any feelings of guilt or shame around money? Around not having enough or earning more than your partner/peers?

_____

_____

Do you save more than you spend or do you spend more than you earn? How does this make you feel?

_____

_____

CAREER

Are you happy with your working life? When you wake up in the morning, how do you feel about what you do every day?

Are you satisfied?

Does what you do every day inspire you?

Are you using your skills adequately?

When you wake up in the morning on a work day, what is your first thought about your day ahead?

If you are in some form of employment, whether you are working for another or yourself, and this job is your source of income, the likelihood is that you spend a significant portion of your life doing it. How you spend your days working to get that paycheck is how you spend a lot of your time, and feeling unhappy, dissatisfied, underappreciated or any other number of negative feelings will have a great influence on your general well-being.

Many of us can feel trapped, by bills, debt and responsibility for others, and changing our situation might not only feel impossible, it might also fill us with fear.

I'm not here to tell you to change anything, but if what you do is eating away at who you are, it might be time to reconsider some of your options.

There is a lot we can do to move forward in our careers, using small, careful steps that will help us feel more appreciated and realise that we can change things without starting again and without giving up anything. Making small changes shows us that change is possible, and all we need sometimes is that glimmer of hope or that seed of experience to see that we are not stuck, that we have far more choice than it might first appear.

One of the things that can get in the way of career goals is something known as 'imposter syndrome'. This stems from a deep-seated, core belief that 'I am not good enough', and I have yet to meet someone, including myself, who hasn't encountered this at some point in their life. It might rear its head when we hear about a better job in work that we are too afraid to apply for. We might feel it whenever we consider changing career and have fear around that. It can appear when we think of doing something totally different, like setting up a business, following our passions or doing what we love. This voice is the voice of fear and the higher the stakes, the louder the fear. Imposter syndrome tells us we can't do it, that we're not good enough, experienced enough, skilled enough or smart enough. Here's the thing, no one is any of those things until they actually get the chance to learn. Everyone has to start somewhere.

So we face a crossroads. We can choose to keep going, carry on as we are and wait for circumstances to change or for opportunity to come knocking on our door. Or we can jump straight in and make it happen for ourselves.

It doesn't mean we have to quit our job and start a full-time four-year degree, but we can find a continuing education programme and study in our free time. We can sign up for a 'Start Your Own Business' course that runs one night per week. We can master our craft, the thing that brings us joy, and seek out a mentor who can inspire us to take it further. Life is full of possibilities and it is up to us to decide that right now is the time, not tomorrow, and to trust that when we follow the path of joy and self-fulfillment, we will find our way.

The reality is that the first time we do something new it won't be our best and, like everything, we will get better with experience. But I can tell you, as someone who has jumped in with two feet many, many times, the first time *will be one of the most special, where you give the very most. It may well be a massive turning point in your life.*

Putting it into action

In the Create section we will work on an exercise that has been instrumental in helping me to find clarity around many areas of my life. Whether I use it for my career and finances, plans or projects, this practical tool always helps me to figure out what is important and gives me a baseline to move forward consciously and with confidence.

We will start to think about our career and our finances by first looking at what our expectations, wants, fears and needs are in relation to these.

By acknowledging what they are, by writing it all down in a list and seeing it in front of us, we can really begin this conversation. We are already driven by our wants, needs, fears and expectations, but this motivation is often done unconsciously, meaning that it is controlling us and not the other way around.

This tool is there to help us figure out what we **want**, what we **need**, what we are **afraid** of and what our inner **expectations** are.

Being clear about what these are will help us to navigate our way around these areas of our lives with order and clarity. It has helped me and I hope it can help you.

WANTS

Wants are our goals and aspirations and the basis for plans.

NEEDS

Needs are non-negotiable.

FEARS

Fears are the things that hold us back.

EXPECTATIONS

Expectations are potential disappointments.

CREATE

Use the space provided to list your expectations, wants, fears and needs surrounding your finances and career based on what you learned in the Contemplate section.

Step 1

List your wants.

I want:

_____

_____

_____

List your needs.

I need … (needs are non-negotiable):

_____

_____

List your fears.

I fear:

_____

_____

_____

List your expectations.

I expect:

_____

_____

_____

Example for finances:

Wants

I want to be able to occasionally treat my partner to a weekend away or a meal.

I want to be able to eat out a few times a week.

I want to be able to save money.

I want to be able to enjoy my life and not worry about money.

Needs

I need to earn enough to cover my rent.

I need to feel financially stable.

I need to save money for a rainy day.

Fears

I fear that I won't be able to pay my credit card bill.

I fear that I will be overdrawn too early in the month.

I fear that unexpected bills like insurance will interfere with my saving plans.

Expectations

I expect to pay my mortgage each month.

I expect to save €300 per month after all my bills and living expenses.

I expect to afford two holidays per year.

Step 2

Shifting expectations

Expectations are potential disappointments and shifting them at this stage allows us to do something about them. For example, 'I expect to pay my mortgage every month' is actually a need. In this case, it is really important and non-negotiable; it will come before everything else if necessary. I've changed it into a need.

The expectation is to save €300 and, in this case, it is a want, a desire. I've changed it below. The last one, 'I expect to afford two holidays per year', is also a want or desire, so I've changed it from an expectation to a want. Once we have shifted all the expectations and moved them into either wants, needs or fears, we can move forward to the next stage of the tool.

Expectations:

    1.   I expect to pay my mortgage each month.

    2.   I expect to save €300 per month after all my bills and living expenses.

    3.   I expect to afford two holidays per year.

Change to:

    1.   I need to pay my mortgage each month.

    2.   I want to save €300 per month after all bills and living expenses.

    3.   I want to afford two holidays per year.

Change all of your expectations into **wants**, **needs** or **fears**. Move them into the section where these are listed and change the first word into 'I want', 'I fear' etc.

For example: 'I expect to be valued for my efforts at work'. When I think about this, it is a need. Under my need list I add 'I need to be valued for my efforts at work'.

Another one: 'I expect that I will not save any money this year' is actually a fear, so I change it to 'I fear that I will not save any money this year' and add it to the bottom of my fear list. By the end of this, all the expectations have shifted into either wants, fears or needs and can then be addressed.

Make SMART goals with your wants and fears. For example, 'I fear I won't be able to pay my bills'. Make a SMART goal that will help you to address this directly, for example: 'Set up a savings account of €x each month.' Review monthly expenses to find areas to save money. Stick with the SMART goal process.

Needs are non-negotiable so list them in the present tense in the form of 'I am …' as an affirmation. For example: 'I need to feel safe and secure in my job – I am safe and secure in my job.' Needs become affirmations that take the top priority in our lives.

I. YOUR FINANCES

Expectations

_____

_____

_____

_____

Wants

_____

_____

_____

_____

Fears

_____

_____

_____

_____

Needs

_____

_____

_____

_____

SMART goals

_____

_____

_____

_____

2. YOUR CAREER

Expectations

_____

_____

_____

_____

Wants

_____

_____

_____

_____

Fears

_____

_____

_____

_____

Needs

_____

_____

_____

_____

SMART goals

_____

_____

_____

_____

Step 3

When you have filled out these two worksheets, one for finances and one for career, look at them together and see what crossovers you can find. Use the Venn diagram below to help you visualise this.

Career 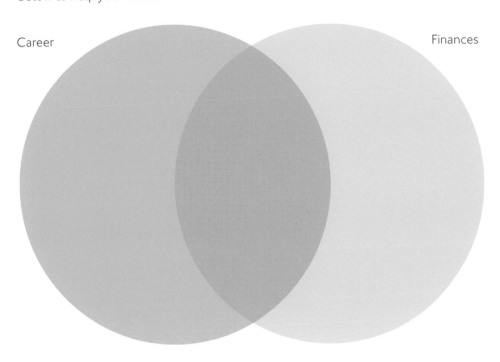 Finances

What do you notice?

_____

Which one is more important for you to work on now?

_____

What are your priorities?

_____

Start to put your SMART goal plans into action plans. Start with the most pressing and important parts first.

MONTHLY REVIEW

Journal a piece on what you have learned about your relationship with your finances and your work. What areas are working well and what areas are not working well yet? Write your feelings around this.

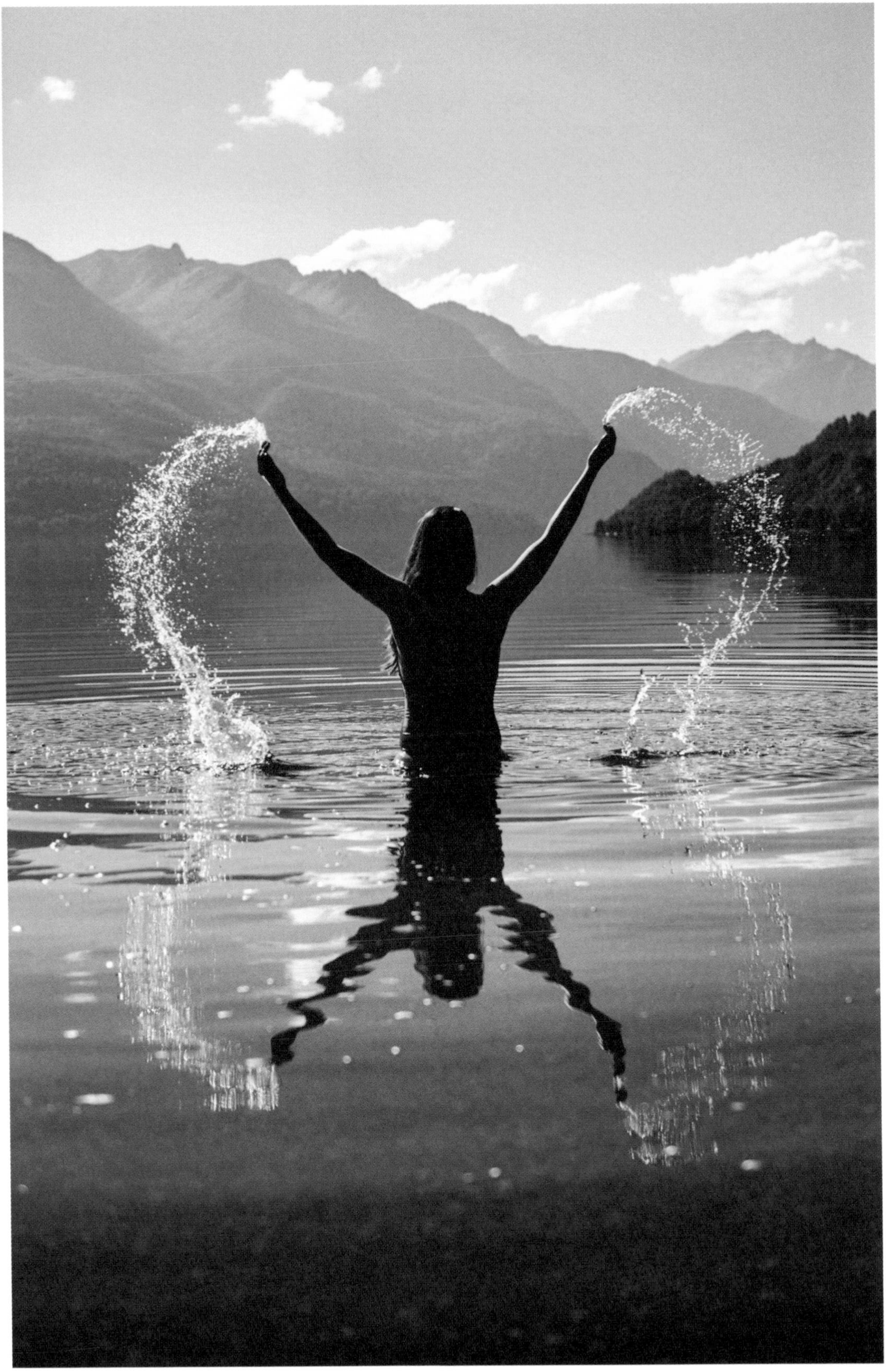

MY NOTES

MY NOTES

MY NOTES

MY NOTES

MY NOTES

MY NOTES

MONTH EIGHT
Compassion – Family and Significant Others

THE GREATEST
OF HUMAN
EMOTIONS
IS LOVE.
THE MOST
VALUABLE OF
HUMAN GIFTS
IS THE ABILITY
TO LEARN.
THEREFORE
LEARN TO LOVE.

– U.J. Ramdas

EXPLORE

In this section we move into the area of the heart and relationships.

It is said that we have three brains: the brain in our head, which is the rational brain we use for analysing and processing; then there's the brain in our gut, which is where we call upon instinct and intuition; and the third brain is our heart – our emotional brain that feels and responds to emotions in the present. Is it any wonder we sometimes struggle with decisions? Each of our brains wants something different!

We might have been offered a job and our head brain is happy as this means we will have enough money to cover the rent and go on a holiday later this year. Our heart brain is struggling as it knows this means giving up on a dream of following a different career path that it desires and the gut brain is sending strange signals as it picked up a weird vibe from our new boss-to-be. It's so interesting.

Compassion is the language of the heart and it is a language worth getting acquainted with. All of our relationships start with ourselves. Whether we have a significant other or are seeking to meet someone. Whether we get along with our family or not. Whether we have a large extended family or whether we are part of a smaller group of people. Our most significant relationships are the ones that teach us the most about how we are, that offer the greatest opportunities for growth, and that shine the mirror of self-reflection back at us.

It all starts with us. We are loved as we love. We are held as we hold. We are cared for as we care. Instead of looking outside of ourselves in this section we will look at how we are. How we cultivate compassion will play a huge part in the important relationships in our life.

Answer the following questions.

1. What family members (extended family too) can you trust?

_____

2. If you're in an intimate relationship, how do you feel about yourself within that relationship?

_____

3. Where would you like to improve your relationship?

_____

4. What's best about your family life?

_____

5. What is it that prevents people from living to their full potential?

_____

6. Write down some acts of kindness that you have received in your lifetime.

_____

7. Are you a caring and compassionate person? Write down some examples.

_____

8. Is it possible to be caring and compassionate to some people and not to others? Can you explain?

_____

9. Describe someone you know who is caring and compassionate.

_____

10. What are the advantages of being a caring and compassionate person?

_____

COMPASSION IS AN ACTION WORD WITH NO BOUNDARIES.

– Prince

What is compassion?

Compassion is a big word and it can mean something different to each of us. It means something on paper but might translate differently in real life. Is compassion a virtue, a quality, a way of life or a feeling? How can compassion fit into our lives? Is it a set thing or can it change depending on the situation?

Compassion became a bigger part of my life when I came to one fundamental realisation. That we are *all* walking around with pain and hurt. That we *all* carry different traumas, that we are *all* suffering.

Yet it can feel like we're completely alone. For those of us with a strong family connection, this can mask the fact that we live our lives on the inside of our own heads, separate from the inside of anyone else's head. Indeed, perhaps living without the true understanding that everyone else is just as much in their own heads as we are: it can sometimes feel like we are alone in that too.

Knowing, really knowing, that we are all in pain – suffering on some level and often on many levels, is when I started to see the world in a different way.

We act from that place of hurt, from the wounds that have befallen us. We react from here too. We have faced traumas and disappointments in our younger years, some more than others. Sometimes the traumas inflicted were unavoidable and happened out of love or survival.

Without healing these traumas, we carry them around and they become the bedrock of who we are, what we are about and are the lens through which we see the world.

Our traumas are our shadow side, the parts of ourselves that have no light shining on it. The pieces of ourselves we relegated to the back of our closet, that we have pushed beneath the surface, but that lurk in the shadows, needing to be set free.

We cannot escape our shadow side; it is a part of who we are. But it is the part of us that is holding us back from who we really are – a shining light of love and potential.

Healing isn't a pleasant, relaxing experience. The real work is when we go deep, bring those feelings, emotions and hurts to the surface, and experience the feelings again as we remember and recall the pain. The very thing we sought to avoid when we buried them.

But our burying does not rid us of the trauma.

Only healing will do that.

And to heal something we have to acknowledge it.

We have to hold it once more. Then we can let it go.

Cultivating compassion

Here are a few strategies and observations to help us bring more compassion into how we live. They require practice and an open mind.

Assumptions

Making an assumption is presuming we understand what someone else means, feels or thinks. We *cannot* know, so there is no point in doing it. Here is an example. A friend had let me down. She had cancelled an appointment, again, to spend some time together. The recent one in particular had left a mark on me and I was starting to take it personally, making the assumption that she didn't want to see me. I resisted further communication and as time went by, I subconsciously created stories in my mind as to why she hadn't made the first move, got back, apologised. Despite not seeing my friend, the situation left me feeling bad, defensive, hurt and feeling self-righteous too. All of these familiar, all of these resonating with past hurts and past pain.

I shook it off. I saw that I was making these assumptions and I shook them off me like a dog getting out of water. I reached out again, genuinely, with no judgement, resentment or bad feelings. She responded back with the same sentiment and we continued our friendship as if the episode hadn't happened.

I had the choice here. I could have either held on to the hurt, demanded she take responsibility for it, or even insisted on an explanation. But all of this was pointing at me, and for whatever reason she let me down, it wasn't about me. I had made that assumption, and if I had held on to it, it would have been a turning point in our relationship. Indeed, I believe we wouldn't actually have a relationship right now if I had. My assumptions would have damaged us both.

I am the person who created this situation by making the assumption and now not only am I the one who is suffering from it, we both are. It is easily done, and often happens when we find we are left short in some way. Looking closer, we may be reacting from a place of hurt, something in the past that triggered the feelings.

Can we drop assumptions by accepting that any number of situations could be occurring at any given moment, and indeed possibly are?

A few more examples

The rude clerk in the shop might have just found out she has a terminal illness and hasn't told anybody.

The impatient driver who is sitting on your tail and then overtakes you in a hurried way may be rushing a sick child to the hospital.

The person in the queue who pushes past you to the till may have just found out her marriage is falling apart.

The uncommunicative teacher at your children's school might be grieving.

When we truly see that there is pain and loss happening all around, we can begin to see that what happens with others isn't about us – it's a reflection of what is happening in their lives.

And it doesn't always have to be the big things. Not getting any sleep because there's an infant in the house or having a sleep disorder can make a working day particularly challenging. A little wisdom to see that it's not 'me', a little compassion to rise above the behaviour and respond with patience, a smile and non-judgement will not only help us to have more peace in our own lives but will help those who are suffering see some light in what might be an otherwise difficult day.

Let them go. Remember that we cannot know what someone else is going through. We are all carrying around our own hurts and pains since birth and some more than others.

PATIENCE, KINDNESS AND COMPASSION ARE THE VIRTUES OF THE WISE.

Expectations

My yoga teacher once told me that all expectations are potential disappointments. This has really stood with me and has been a huge help in my life. Expectations *are* potential disappointments. They are a little like assumptions: we assume something is going to happen in a certain way.

Expectations assume control of an outcome – again, our logical brain knows this isn't ever possible. There are so many possible outcomes for any one situation and attaching ourselves to one will most certainly lead to disappointment on our behalf.

Keep an open mind. Let that shit go.

If we expect something to finish with a particular outcome, then work with the expectation to make it a goal. Change the expectation into a plan. Then at least we have some control over the outcome.

But an expectation without a plan is simply a disappointment in waiting. Can you drop your expectations and start to approach things with an open mind?

For example, a family holiday or celebration. History and repetition can lead us to create expectations around things that have happened before a certain way. We may expect for this event to be amazing and magical like it was before. Just as each day is different, we are also different, and with varying circumstances no two events, no two holidays, will be the same.

Having strong expectations not only puts additional pressure on the situation before it even happens, but the expectations will most likely become disappointments as we have no power to predict how something will go.

Dropping our expectations as an actual practice, as an intention, can really help us to have a more relaxed approach to what may be and stay in the present moment with what is.

Knowing we want to let go of expectations and actually doing it is a different thing entirely. We can use the Law of Attraction to bring these thoughts into the physical realm. Let me explain. The Law of Attraction states that our thoughts create our reality and that what we focus on in our minds we attract into our lives. It is always working, like gravity, it is happening with or without our awareness. What is interesting is that it isn't purely what we think that causes the attraction, but what we feel. Thoughts create feelings, but we have so many thousands of thoughts during our waking hours that unless we are conscious with them, especially when it comes to how they make us feel, then we are not working with this principal. It is working us. Focus on what you want. Think about it consciously and begin to 'feel' those thoughts in your body, in your whole being. That is how we use the Law of Attraction. We can speak the words out loud or in our head or write them down as an intention. It can seem unnatural and disingenuous at first but like anything, the more we practise the easier it becomes.

We can repeat the intention as many times as we need to before we start to feel our thoughts shifting. We can revisit it often and, when something is really important, we can place it somewhere we can see it and be reminded of it often.

For example

My intention for this [holiday/Christmas/birthday] is to let go of any expectations I have and to go into the experience with an open mind and open heart. I will remain present, allowing the events to unfold naturally and let go of any comparisons to previous years. I am grateful for the opportunity to spend time with loved ones and will release any expectations I may be harbouring.

Celebrate others' success

Linked closely to the Law of Attraction but also important in its own right is the idea of celebrating the successes of others.

In a world where we may be struggling with any aspect of our own life, whether that's popularity and our social scene, our professional life and finances, our home and family situation or how we look and perceive physical appearance, we may find we compare ourselves to others.

Self-worth, self-esteem and our general confidence is closely linked to our past and the experiences we had when we were younger. Subconsciously, we find we perceive ourselves through comparison to others, whether that's someone we know or someone we see online.

When we feel a lack of self-worth about our self, it can easily manifest as judgement or criticism of another. For example, someone at work got a big promotion and it highlights our own insecurity about our career. We might find we are being negative around that person's success out of a fear or doubt about our own life.

This is where the Law of Attraction comes into play and, whatever our motive for feeling negative around another's success, the fact is these feelings do not serve us, nor do they bring abundance banging on our door.

If you catch yourself in this situation, immediately reframe it. Change your feelings around. Do a 180 and wish them well. Say it out loud if you like but most importantly – think it.

Good for her. Well done her. She deserves it.

It takes practice. I remember well the cattiness of teenage girls and the 'who do you think you are' attitude I came up against in my youth. I hope that this has dissipated with time. I'm certainly still working on it.

We need to support each other and one of the ways we can start to do that is to celebrate other people's successes, even if your initial reaction wasn't to feel that.

Change it. Wish them well. The universe is listening.

LOOKING AT THINGS
FROM OTHER PEOPLE'S
POINT OF VIEW IS
PRACTICALLY THE SECRET
OF SUCCESS.

– Paul Graham

Forgiveness

A simple word, something that resonates deep within all of us, but one of the hardest steps on our healing journey.

There is no clear path to forgiveness. We may find we can forgive to a certain degree but are just not ready to forgive certain grievances. No one can *tell* us to forgive, certainly no one has the power to *make* us forgive. This is without doubt a solo journey and a large, vital step on the journey to self-peace.

FORGIVING SOMEONE DOES NOT MEAN THAT WE CONDONE THEIR ACTIONS.

FORGIVING SOMEONE MEANS WE ARE NO LONGER HARBOURING THOSE FEELINGS INSIDE US.

FORGIVENESS IS RELEASING THE PAIN, THE EMOTION AND THE ENERGY.

IT IS ONLY SOMETHING THAT WE CAN DO WHEN WE ARE READY.

If you are struggling with forgiving someone or harbouring a grievance for another, here is a practical tool to try. The first question to ask is: Am I ready to forgive them?

If the answer is yes – great!

Ask yourself what the life lesson was from the situation. What have you learned from this? What has it taught you? These situations, where there is conflict with another, are usually painful and uncomfortable.

What did you learn? For example, I am angry at someone for mistreating me and for not showing me respect. I am ready to forgive that person and to let it go. My life lesson is to seek that forgiveness of myself for allowing myself to be disrespected. That I accepted the behaviour and didn't stand up for myself.

If the answer is no, then consider this:

What are you gaining by holding on to this anger? If there is a situation where you have a grievance for someone and it doesn't seem to go away you could try this: Send blessings to them for 30 days. You can do this with prayer or intention. After 30 days things will either have resolved the situation or you won't care anymore.

Empathy

Before we look at what empathy *is*, let's first look at what it *is not*.

We'll start with an example. In this situation let's pretend that a friend has come to you in distress as she has just found out her partner is having an affair and is going to leave her.

Please feel free to substitute this with another situation that feels appropriate – what is important is that someone has come to you to share her distress. She is hurt, struggling, and is suffering in her pain. The following table shows some of the typical ways that we as humans respond to situations. We are often uncomfortable with someone else's pain.

ADVISING	giving advice to help them.
ANALYSING	looking at the situation from an investigatory perspective to gain thorough knowledge of all sides.
COMPARING	sharing a similar story, either yours or someone else's.
CORRECTING	interrupting a person to correct a detail that you know to be inaccurate.
COUNSELLING	using your knowledge or skills to counsel them in their situation.
DATA-GATHERING	interrupting to ask questions and gather details (when? how? where).
DIAGNOSING	giving an opinion on the situation from your perspective.
DISCOUNTING	steering the situation to make it seem less bad than it is.
EDUCATING	using the situation as an opportunity to help the person to learn a lesson.
FIXING	doing anything to help the situation and make it go away.
ONE-UPPING	sharing your own story that's far worse.
REASSURING	telling the person that it's going to get better, that it will be ok.
SILVER-LINING	putting a plaster on it and pretending it isn't so bad, saying 'at least you have your friends/great job etc.'.
SYMPATHISING	feeling sorry for the person.

I'm sure that if we are really honest with ourselves, we will find that we have used some of these approaches in our lives. To be clear, none of these are empathy.

What is empathy? Think about it for a minute. When a person is in distress and comes to us to share her story, firstly it is a great privilege to be that someone she wants around her in her time of difficulty. The situation here is about her. She needs to share, to talk and to express her thoughts and feelings.

In any of the previous situations the reaction is not about her, it is about the listener.

Read through them again. They all turn the arrow of focus back on us, as we consider our reaction to the situation.

Yet the situation is not about us, it is and should always be about her. We love this person, we want to do the best thing for her, so why do we fall into one of these responses?

Three reasons:

One: it is uncomfortable to be with someone who is hurting and it is our impulse to help her. We do not want to see anyone in pain.

Two: we are uncomfortable with not saying anything and not doing anything, we haven't been taught how to hold space for someone who is hurting.

Three: many of us grew up in a world where we were not supposed to show our emotions, where we do not cry, especially in public and especially if we are male.

Empathy is listening

It doesn't mean that we just sit there mute. When we listen, we do so in a way that is called active listening. Which means that 100 per cent of our awareness is on that person. We listen with every cell in our body with our attention fully on that person. No phone, no moaning kids, no TV could distract us, we are *really* present in that moment and *fully with* that person.

And that person will know it.

And she will feel seen and heard. And that is what she needs.

It is what we all need.

You might say that our greatest need is love, and this may well be true. But the act of truly seeing a person for who she is, to really listen to that person, true, deep listening – that is the greatest act of love.

We also need food, water and shelter of course, but just as living without those reduces our chances of survival, in a world where we are not seen and not heard, we will not be really living.

Holding space for someone, really seeing them and listening to them is the greatest gift we can give. It takes practice. We are busier, more distracted, faster and less present in the modern day, but learning to listen deeply is something we can practice. Once we have done it a few times and experienced first-hand the effects it has on another, we will know that this is the way.

Love

Love is the highest vibration and the highest form of all consciousness.

We feel love for our family, our pets and our friends. We may not always know it but the grief we feel at the loss of loved ones is a true measure of the love we feel for them.

Love is boundless and eternal and it doesn't dissipate over time. We do not love a parent/sibling/child any less as the years since their passing amass. The memories and the visuals of that person may become less clear but the love does not change nor go away.

TIME CAN FEEL LINEAR AS WE GO THROUGH LIFE, BUT WHEN IT COMES TO LOVE, TIME IS CYCLICAL AND CIRCULAR.

It is not an unfamiliar feeling to love our family more than anyone else. Family is sacred. And when love for a significant other becomes just as strong, we bring them into our family unit, and they do the same. We cohabit and share a life with that person, within the tight family unit.

Love for our friends is also real and strong. It may not contain the physical closeness of our immediate family, and we may or may not verbalise our feelings, yet love for our friends is present in varying degrees.

Love for our pets is another area where we can recognise this feeling. Most of us have witnessed the strong bond between man and animal at some point in our lives.

Love for strangers. If love is the highest vibration of all, and is our natural state, is it selective and only for those close to us? When a tragedy happens and the news channels are streaming the images and footage 24/7 and we see the pain and suffering in front of our eyes, I believe we are feeling love for those people. When we allow, even for a moment, their pain to enter into our physical space, we are perceiving the true weight of their loss. It is a heavy load. But many of us do this. We feel this.

THIS HELPS US TO SEE THAT LOVE
IS OUR NATURAL STATE.

TO FEEL LOVE FOR STRANGERS.
PEOPLE LIVING DIFFERENT LIVES
TO US.

WE DO HAVE LOVE FOR ALL
BEINGS.

IT IS WHO WE ARE.

IT IS WHAT WE ARE.

LOVE.

CREATE

Write down a list of all the people you love. Can you find a way to let them know how you feel? It will be different from person to person. Perhaps a letter, a card, a phone call or a text. Make a plan to let the people you love know how important they are to you.

Make it your mission this month to have some communication with each of the people who mean the most to you. Perhaps that's a special date with a significant other. Perhaps it's some one-on-one time with your child or each of your children. Perhaps it's a scheduled phone call with a friend or family member living abroad.

MONTHLY REVIEW

What was your big take-home this month?

_____

_____

_____

_____

_____

_____

How do you think you can start to integrate the teachings into your life more?

_____

_____

_____

_____

_____

_____

_____

MY NOTES

MY NOTES

MY NOTES

MY NOTES

MY NOTES

MY NOTES

MONTH NINE
Community and Friends

EXPLORE

Welcome to Month Nine. You are doing amazing work in whatever form and whatever direction it is taking you. Even committing to as little as an hour a month or 15 minutes a week has great value and, as life is never the same from day to day, we might find we ebb and flow with this work. Trust the process and know that you are doing great. If you have veered off-piste you can pick it up again at any time.

In this section we explore our community and friendships. As human beings we have a deep sense of belonging and in the context of life we are always seeking connection with other people who are going through life along with us. It would be a very isolating experience otherwise and not only do we learn from each other but we need each other for support, encouragement and fun. In a community we balance each other with our varying gifts, skill and strengths, and the uniqueness of each individual means we are always learning and being inspired by each other.

Understanding who is important to me

Which of your friends are most important to you?

_____

_____

_____

Write down the names of three people in your life with whom you can be completely honest and say anything you like.

1. _____

2. _____

3. _____

What do you want most in a friend?

_____

_____

What values are important to you in friendship?

_____

_____

Who are the friends that make you feel the best about yourself?

_____

_____

Who are the people in your life you can depend on?

_____

_____

What's your social life like?

_____

_____

_____

_____

What would you like to change and improve on?

_____

_____

_____

_____

Could your relationships be deeper, more rewarding and more meaningful?

_____

_____

_____

_____

To truly be in service

The gift of giving has long been known as one of the surest ways to peace and happiness. The story of the Good Samaritan has been told in many variations in countries, cultures and religions all around the world. I have experienced some of the most heartfelt generosity while travelling in countries less developed than my own and received kindness and many meals from people who looked like they didn't have anything to spare. It is an age-old truth that people who have the least give the most.

TIME IS THE GREATEST GIFT WE HAVE TO GIVE.

Giving and doing what is right speaks to the very heart of who we are and what we believe in. What we believe in and what we do are not always congruous with each other. We might feel a certain way about something, but we do not act on it – this refers to authenticity. Authenticity is when we say and do what we actually believe. Being authentic is an essential part of trusting, allowing and loving who we are, and being confident enough to let that shine.

Our actions will not always be in agreement with others. We will not be able to keep everyone happy: 'To avoid criticism, say nothing, do nothing, be nothing' (Fred Shero).

But when we are being authentic our path is aligned with who we are and this removes blockages, releases fears and we become stronger in knowing what we want.

In our heart, we are kind, loving beings who do not wish others to suffer and who long for peace. When we came into the world, we were pure love, and that love has not gone away, despite being buried in the traumas of life. Connecting to our compassionate, loving selves is bringing ourselves into a more authentic space. Being of service, through the gift of giving, is one of the purest forms of love.

The ancient yogis talked a lot about service. It is referred to as Karma or Seva yoga and is described as selfless service. The selfless part refers to attachment to the outcome, meaning the act is entirely focused outwards. For an act to be purely selfless, this extends to even the simple fact of feeling good about helping another.

In this case, the focus turns back on the self, and part of the outcome is now about the giver – about how the giver feels. This is a very challenging concept to understand as no matter how noble our intentions, it is hard to not be attached to any results of our benevolent assistance. It is such a simple yet challenging concept that it is at the heart of one of the most illustrious and sacred of ancient Indian and yogic texts, the *Bhagavad Gita*.

BEING A GIVER DOESN'T REQUIRE EXTRAORDINARY ACTS OF SACRIFICE. IT JUST INVOLVES A FOCUS ON ACTING IN THE INTERESTS OF OTHERS.

– Adam M. Grant

Our intention

We may think that whether or not we *feel* good about it bears no relevance on the person or situation we are helping. If we are offering our service, helping someone or a cause – if we are *doing* it, does it matter what our intention is?

Here's the thing. It does. Why is this?

When we are truly being of service to another (or the environment, an animal, a cause) and our pure and whole intention is to offer help in the best way possible for that person, we are moving from the inside out, we are the subject and they are the object.

When we are doing something for another with either a conscious or subconscious intention to make ourselves feel better, then we are doing it from the outside in, we become the object and they become the subject. What intention does here, is that the energy is directed inward, not outward, and the outcome is focused on the doer.

When we are kind and loving and focus on what is right and authentic to us, magic happens. This magic ripples out into the world with far-reaching effects beyond our own imaginings. Like a pebble dropped into a pond, the waves travel outwards and become exponentially bigger. When we are focused on ourselves and our giving is self-orientated, the waves travel inwards and stop abruptly with nowhere else to go. The magic ends there.

One amazing example of this type of giving is the generosity of William Tyrone Guthrie. A successful theatre director and lover of the arts, he died in 1971, leaving his manor home to the Irish State as a residential workplace for artists. The sole stipulation in his will was that all residents share a meal together in the evening. Ten years after he died at home at Annaghmakerrig, the Tyrone Guthrie Centre was opened. This was achieved with the hard work, vision and commitment of Arts Councils on both sides of the border, at a time of deep political division. The centre has grown and developed with the acquisition of land and additional accommodation and is now a sought-after retreat for writers, artists and performers from around the world, the shared meal being an integral part of the experience.

When Tyrone died, he did not know the massive impact this would continue to have. Not just in the inspiration and focus it provides to artists, not just for the many people who get to read the writing, look at the paintings, listen to the music, but to that one person. That one person for whom, while observing art that was created there, has something stirred deep inside of them. Something that changes their lives, their outlook and who they are. This is the magic. The magic we are too limited to imagine, too self-absorbed to visualise. This is the magic that the universe conjures up when we are willing and ready to offer our gifts without any attachment. When our intention is pure, magic happens that is beyond our limited imagination.

A SOCIETY GROWS
GREAT WHEN OLD MEN
PLANT TREES IN WHOSE
SHADE THEY KNOW THEY
SHALL NEVER SIT.

– Greek proverb

Better together

One of the main ideas behind this book was to create a manual for leading a balanced life that would be empowering, accessible and supportive. Willpower and discipline are necessary but will only get us so far. After that there needs to be something spurring us along if we want to sustain these healthy practices, and joy is a great motivator.

Here's where friends come in – perhaps the health practice in question may not feel so joyful, especially at first, but doing it with people *who make us happy* puts a new spin on things. Doing healthy, positive and active things with friends and family has three important benefits.

Accountability – Recognised across many fields as the missing link to positive habit follow-through, this is probably the main reason to consider hooking up with like-minded people to get active. Whether you have planned a run, a walk or hike, a swim or a workout or class, you're a lot less likely to shirk off if you have arranged to do it with someone else.

It is easy for the voices in our heads to tell us it's too cold/too early/too much work to do/not enough time – there are endless excuses our minds will find to stop us from following through. Once the plan has been made, and we know that person will be standing there waiting for us, it is usually enough of a catalyst in those crucial seconds after the alarm has gone off to actually get out of bed instead of abandoning all the previous night's intentions in favour of sleep.

It is useful during the day, too, when the momentum of doing can make our sound intentions of 'making it to the pool' seem inaccessible under the weight of busyness. If there is someone expecting us to show up at a prearranged time, we will make room for that in our day.

Likewise, in the evening, we might feel too tired and use that as our excuse not to head back outside again, but a friend who is waiting will ensure we find the extra energy for one more hour.

We are up against a huge battle when we go it solo, the battle of our own mind, and pound for pound it's a tough call who'll win. It could go either way. Bringing that simple element of 'someone else' into the equation makes it easier as there is no thinking, procrastinating, excuse-making or deliberating. We make the plan and we stick to it. And if we cancel, it's for a legitimate reason. Easy.

Progress – Being active with someone else means we get to experience their levels, abilities and limits. Perhaps you are comfortable with a 3 km run, but your buddy prefers 5 km. You might find initially that you run to your pace, but the goal will be there to increase this in order to catch up with her. We learn a lot from each other in so many ways, and the more we are active with different people, the more likely we are to see things differently and begin to want to experience things differently too.

Connection – Not to be overlooked, this obvious benefit might also be the most important. Where people live the longest and healthiest lives, there is a unanimous spirit of connection and relationship within the communities across all the countries. Life can feel isolating at times, and the bond between people doing something that makes them feel alive and vibrant is a great thing to experience. Even if the relationships don't extend beyond the activity, it exists and is rewarding and healing. Meeting people who enjoy what you do, and who want to look after their body and mind, is a great motivator to keep going. Making new friends at any stage of life is a gift.

SETTING UP A HEALTHY NETWORK

The main thing to do is to decide what it is you want to do.

This is the hard part, and yet this is something you are absolutely capable of doing.

What brings you joy? What feels amazing in your body?

Do you get excited about the idea of going to the gym?

Do you feel free when you run?

Do you feel alive when you swim in the pool, or out in wild water somewhere?

Do you crave the discipline of a set class led by an instructor?

Do you love to walk or hike in nature, a park or by the ocean?

Do you enjoy the climbing wall, the bike or the boxing ring?

What form of active movement gets you excited?

Does a round of golf with a friend sound like the perfect day?

Once you've decided what it is you want to do, you're halfway there. You just need someone else to join you. Put it out to friends. Everyone wants to be healthy and vibrant, everyone wants to be their best selves, and we are all struggling with the same issues of commitment, discipline and procrastination. It won't be hard to find someone. Once you have someone, it will snowball from there. Perhaps you want to keep it small and intimate, or perhaps you want to open it up to a larger group. There are benefits to both.

Rise fierce

One cold winter's morning in 2017, a group of women met on the beach in Lahinch, a small seaside village on the west coast of Ireland. It was cold, wet, windy and the tide was a long way out. We stripped down to our swimmers and walked across the sand to the water's edge. Our skin pink and vulnerable against the pale winter's light, our faces creased from our pillows while the world was still stirring in their beds. Every one of us wondering what the hell we were doing as we reluctantly plunged into the freezing water. As we emerged, the energy was changed. We were charged, inflated, laughing and joyful. Turns out doing something challenging and powerful can really make us feel alive.

We have kept the 7.30 a.m. swimming going and since then the WhatsApp group created grows every day. There are groups of women swimming every day, all year, at different times of the day in different places along this small stretch of coast, connecting on an app and sharing this together. It is changing the lives of the people who swim and friendships are forming and bonds are being forged. As the years go by the group has become something different and no doubt will continue to morph but the beauty is that it is reaching more and more people and bringing something positive to more and more lives. What started as a small idea – I wanted to be a daily sea swimmer – has taken on a life of its own.

All I did to start with was to talk about it. From that one little action – knowing what I wanted – it has snowballed beyond my imagination and is no longer about me, although I greatly benefit from it every day. One of the original swimmers, a surfer and environmentalist using her social-media influence for positive change, started attaching the hashtag #risefierce to our daily swims and that tag has begun to inspire women all over the world to get into cold water. It's incredible what can happen when we dare to dream about what we want, and are then brave enough to put it out there and share our thoughts with others. We can move mountains.

Is there something you would like to do, something that gets you moving and brings you back into nature? Perhaps there is something that will help you break a sedentary cycle, but you can't find the motivation to start? Find a friend, and in a few years' time, who knows? You might just have pioneered a little movement in your own environment that is helping people in ways you never imagined.

CREATE

Set up a healthy network doing something fun, rewarding and good for you.

Draft one person or a dozen people if you prefer. Call them on the phone or set up a group on a social-media platform.

Integrate doing something positive for *yourself* such as exercise, or helping the environment with a beach clean, with spending time with like-minded people who make you feel good.

Write down three ideas for a healthy network:

1. _____

2. _____

3. _____

Which one are you most drawn to? Use your SMART goals to put this plan into action. Start now!

MONTHLY REVIEW

What has this month shown you with regard to who is important in your life?

_____

_____

_____

Do you think community is important? Think about how community differs to friendship and explore why this connection is important in our lives.

_____

_____

_____

What community projects are there in your area? Do some research and find out what initiatives are happening around you.

_____

_____

_____

How can you get involved in your community more? Write down three ways you can contribute.

1. _____

2. _____

3. _____

Write down three ways in which you would benefit from this.

1. _____

2. _____

3. _____

Who are the marginalised people in your community? Is it the elderly, the homeless, the sick?

_____

_____

Think about something you could do with a friend that would not only contribute to your community but bond the two of you together and give you time with each other. What would you need to do to make this happen?

_____

_____

_____

MY NOTES

MY NOTES

MY NOTES

MY NOTES

MY NOTES

MY NOTES

MONTH TEN
Play – Fun and Recreation

EXPLORE

Making Space for What I Love

Do you make time for fun in your life? For the things you love? Do you remember a time when you used to laugh a lot more than you do now? At certain times in our life we might find it hard to make time for fun as routine, work and the responsibility of caring for others bring us into a life that doesn't always prioritise joy and fun for us. It doesn't mean we have to change everything to start to bring in more of what makes us happy. The Contemplate section explores what is means to touch life directly and have really meaningful experiences first-hand. This is a way to cultivate joy and it brings us back to the very essence of who we really are.

I hope you find these sections confronting and useful!

THOSE WHO PLAY
RARELY BECOME
BRITTLE IN THE
FACE OF STRESS OR
LOSE THE HEALING
CAPACITY FOR
HUMOUR.

– Stuart Brown MD

Answer the following questions.

Write down three things that you love doing. It could be sport, a hobby, an activity etc.

1. _____

2. _____

3. _____

What makes you forget to eat?

_____

_____

Why do you love these things? How do they make you feel?

_____

_____

How long do you spend doing each? Think in terms of weekly or monthly.

_____

_____

What would need to happen for you to be able to find more time for these things?

_____

_____

Remember back to when you were a child. What did you find fun then? Write about a time you distinctly remember having fun. Describe it. How does it feel now?

How do the things you own enhance your life?

How do the things you own detract from your life?

CONTEMPLATE

First-hand experience

What does it mean to be alive? To really live?

What if the meaning of life was simply to live?

The great British philosopher Alan Watts said that just as the ocean waves, the universe peoples. In other words, we are an expression of the universe and the act of living is the purpose of life. What does *living* mean? Does it matter, aren't we all living? Or is there a better way to live than how we are living?

Is being perpetually busy a natural human state? Cut off from nature, spending the majority of our day inside, working, staring into a screen – is this really living? We all know the answer to that. Yet turning it all around is daunting and we are not going to simply upend our life, walk away from everything and start over. For the record, I am not recommending this!

> # IF WE ARE TRUDGING THROUGH LIFE IGNORING THE TRUTH, WHAT IS IMPORTANT TO US, WHAT WE NEED AND WHAT BRINGS US ALIVE, LIFE WILL FIND A WAY TO SHOW US.

There is a way we can begin to piece our priorities back together, piece by piece, and that is to come in direct contact with life again. Like we did when we were children. With the thrill, the wonder and the majesty of getting close to the source – to nature – we can reach out and touch life first-hand.

Touching life directly

What does that look like for you?

Is it a walk on a cold windy day on an isolated beach? Is it watching a sunset from a hilltop that pushed and challenged your body and mind to reach its summit? Is it getting into a body of open water and beating your fears and doubts to do it? Could it be braving something new, being out of your comfort zone while being in nature like surfing, running, climbing or kayaking? Is it getting up early, despite the voice in your head, to bring yourself to a beautiful place, alone, to watch a sunrise?

This is the simplicity of living in its purest form.

Doing something that makes you feel ALIVE.

This will bring us back to what's important.

SLOWLY AND SURELY OUR
CONNECTION WITH LIFE WILL
REASSURE US OF OUR PLACE ON
THIS EARTH. SLOWLY AND SURELY
OUR CONNECTION WITH THE
EARTH WILL REASSURE US OF
OUR PLACE IN LIFE.

Play, laughter and joy are ways to touch life directly. We only have to watch children to remember that. This was our way. We were children. We knew how to surrender to the moment and live it as purely and perfectly as the rain falls and the rivers run. Coming back to real experiences reminds us of our childhood and our eternal understanding of what our nature really is.

SIMPLICITY, PATIENCE, COMPASSION. THESE THREE ARE YOUR GREATEST TREASURES. SIMPLE IN ACTIONS AND THOUGHTS, YOU RETURN TO THE SOURCE OF BEING.
PATIENT WITH BOTH FRIENDS AND ENEMIES, YOU ACCORD WITH THE WAY THINGS ARE. COMPASSIONATE TOWARD YOURSELF, YOU RECONCILE ALL BEINGS IN THE WORLD.

– Lao Tzu

Dancing

Dance every chance you get! Even if we feel self-conscious letting loose on the dance floor, our body and our soul loves it! Allowing our body to move in any direction and doing this to music we love is an absolute tonic. Dance as much as you can. Dance in your kitchen, dance in the morning or head out for a night of dancing on the tiles with your pals. Just dance! It's such a hugely healing expression for the body and literally fills us with joy from tip to toe. If you're not finding joy in dancing then perhaps it's time to revisit this. Start by playing your favourite dance tunes at home on your own and dance away by yourself. Even a five-minute kitchen dance party has the power to boost your mood and make you smile.

Happy with less: how decluttering your home can create space for play and creativity

While it's not exactly news that our overconsumption is affecting the planet in a serious way, what we might not realise is that our overconsumption affects us on a personal level too. According to the ancient Chinese practice of feng shui, clutter in our homes causes stagnation and stops a flow of chi (energy) from circulating in a healthy way. This affects our physical, mental and emotional health. In short, our living space reflects how we feel. When we declutter and clear out, we feel lighter and sleep better.

Clearing out our home creates space both physically and mentally. For example, it is hard for me to envision getting down on my hands and playing fun games with my kids in a living space that is full of stuff, has no clear counters and a lot of laundry calling out for me to do. When we make space in our surroundings, we also pave the way for simple living – living that naturally brings us back to the source, back to who we are and back to what's important. Instinctually we know that play and freedom of expression are important but our never-ending to-do list takes precedent in a home that is weighed down by too much stuff.

Many of us are hoarders, a habit we may have picked up from our parents and they from theirs. Things can weigh us down and letting go of some of our possessions can literally lighten our load. But where do we start?

Here are some tips to get you going:

1. Take a leaf out of author and declutterer Marie Kondo's book: if it doesn't spark joy, it's time to say goodbye. I would add, keep it if it's useful: you might have a sieve that doesn't spark joy but that you use most days, so hang on to it. Just make sure you don't have several of them!

2. Start small. For many of us, the task of decluttering is a daunting prospect. Start with one drawer and completely finish this one place before starting on another. Set a realistic goal for working your way through your home, one drawer, shelf or cupboard at a time.

3. Repurpose, re-gift, recycle – ensure you're not simply dumping everything into the bin. Charity shops will gladly take your clothes. Crèches and playschools may be interested in used but unbroken toys. Second-hand bookshops will take books. Check with local charities. Where I live there is a private Facebook page on which people give their unused items away for free and things get snapped up very fast. It just requires a photo and some planning. Friends may want some of the things. It takes more effort than simply throwing stuff away but you will feel a lot better doing it this way.

4. Re-gifting. It can be hard to part with something that was given as a gift, as you may feel guilty doing so. But if you don't use it, want it or need it then it is not only taking up space in your home, it isn't serving its purpose. Re-gifting it to someone else means that the item has served its purpose of being a wanted gift. Don't feel guilty. Give it away as a gift again.

5. Be realistic. Do you really need that many same-sized saucepans, that number of mugs? Try to gauge what you really need. Be ruthless. You will feel calmer and happier in a less cluttered environment.

6. Once you've made a decision to move stuff along, do it quickly. Don't leave it around for you to change your mind! Take it step by step, one shelf at a time until it's fully cleared and reorganised. And deal with the unwanted stuff at once, or else you'll be living with piles of stuff on the floor instead of on shelves or in cupboards.

7. Clothes can be tricky. Try to only keep the ones that spark the most joy. And unless you think you will wear a piece of clothing 30 times, don't buy it. Unethical clothing industries are not only harmful to our planet, they are harmful to the people making the clothing. The price of wasteful clothing consumption, spawned by the advent of the cheap mass-producers, has finally come to light. The effects are devastating. Think carefully. Do you really need it? Where was it made? Who made it?

8. Experiences over things. As a family we made the decision to choose experiences over things. That is, to gift activities, travel and adventures

over something we can box wrap. With children that isn't always possible, especially at Christmas and birthdays, but where we can we choose an experience, something we can do together, over bringing another item into our home.

9. One in, one out. This is one of the hardest rules and I'd be lying if I said I stuck to this all the time – if I did, I wouldn't need to spend time decluttering! Stuff comes into our home all the time. Gifts, kids' art from school, non-perishable food items … If we are not processing an equal amount of stuff out with the same frequency, then we will very quickly find ourselves accumulating too much. Having too much of anything not only means we can't find what we need, we often don't even know what we have. It's a habit, and if we are not in control of this, over time it can lead to a hoarding mentality. We can become attached to our things, thinking we need them. But the reality is, we really don't need very much at all.

10. The best thing that has happened since I've embraced a more minimal life is that I really think twice before buying new things. I am more conscious of packaging when I make my purchases and creating space to question whether I 'really need it' has helped me to buy less. My home is less cluttered, easier to clean and I have more disposable income as a result.

HOLDING ON TO THINGS IS SIGNALLING TO THE UNIVERSE THAT YOU DON'T BELIEVE YOU WILL BE PROVIDED FOR WHEN YOU WILL ACTUALLY NEED IT.

Would you benefit from a declutter?

_____

_____

_____

Do you consider yourself a hoarder?

_____

_____

_____

Where in your life could you cut back on what you buy?

_____

_____

Think about the ways you could minimise consumption and give it a go. Good luck! It might be a lot deeper and more profound than you think.

_____

_____

_____

_____

_____

CREATE

Write down four things that you can do that will bring you into a state of play and laughter. Get creative. It might be to visit a comedy club. It might be to sign up for something fun like ice-skating, or more challenging, like a climbing course. Think about activities that bring an element of play, fun and laughter. It might be a night out dancing with your friends. Or even a night of board and card games at home with the family! Commit to doing one thing a week that is devoted to joy. Journal about it afterwards. How did it feel?

1. _____

2. _____

3. _____

4. _____

Use your SMART goals to create a plan to start decluttering your home. Start small and notice how lightening your load gives you space on the inside and out.

MONTHLY REVIEW

What have you learned about yourself this month?

_____

_____

_____

_____

_____

_____

_____

_____

_____

_____

_____

_____

_____

What three things from this month would you like to bring forward with you?

1. _____

2. _____

3. _____

MY NOTES

MY NOTES

MY NOTES

MY NOTES

MY NOTES

MY NOTES

MONTH ELEVEN
Spirituality

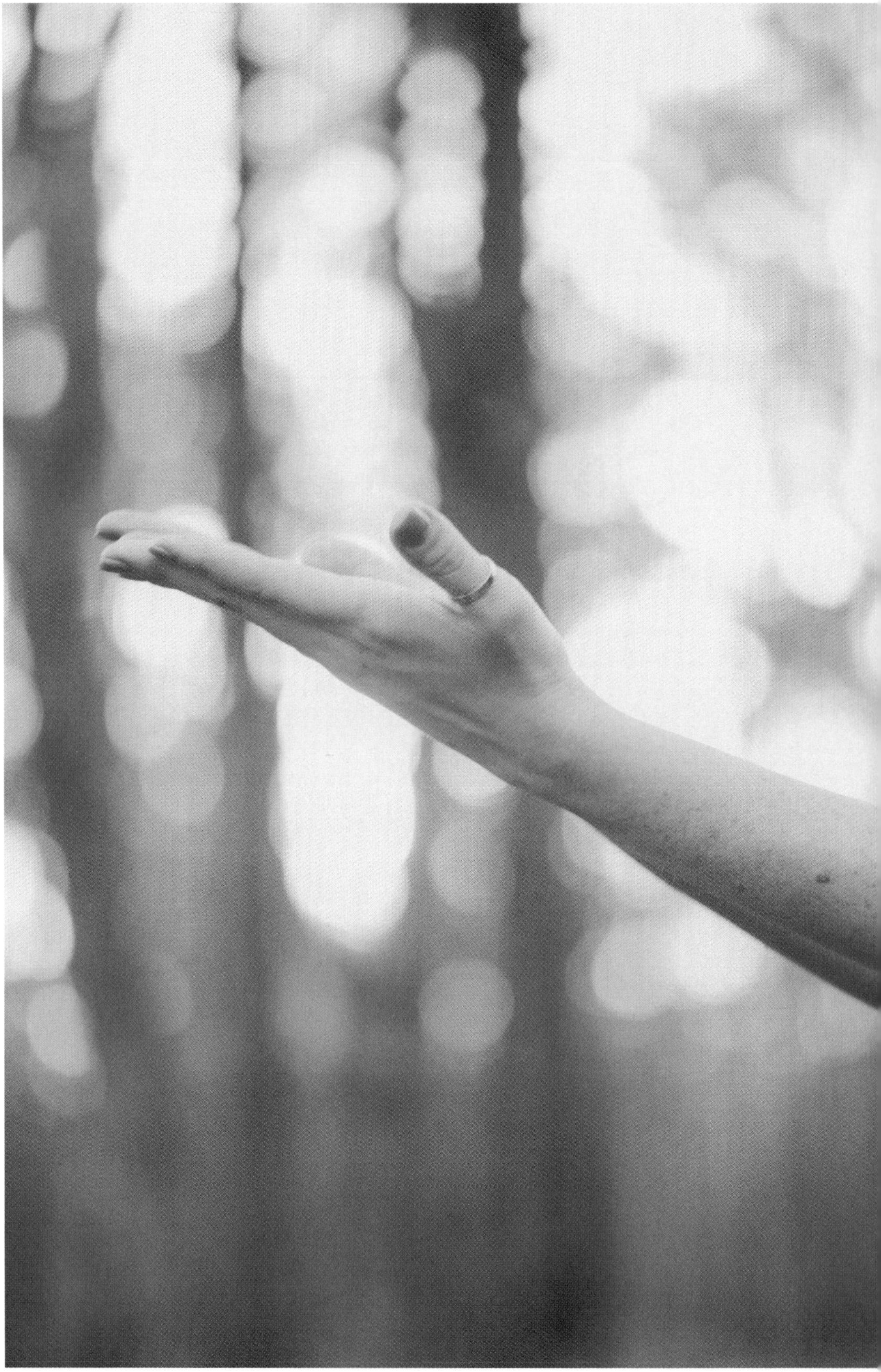

EXPLORE

This month we will begin to explore what 'spirituality' means to us and to our connection to life. The questions in this section explore some deep subjects and themes and each deserves some time. I would recommend limiting your answers to one a day or one every two days to really focus on this. Remember, there is no right or wrong answer for these questions, we are simply bringing our awareness inwards to find some deep answers to some big questions.

The Contemplate section brings some of my experience as a yoga and meditation teacher to the table. I went to my first yoga class when I was 21 and living a busy life as an English teacher in the middle of Hong Kong. I was young and fit and while some of it was challenging, I was able to make it through the physical portion of the class, albeit slightly confused as to what we were doing. At the end of the class the teacher set us up for a really long relaxation. She turned off the lights, lit candles and burned incense. She gave us blankets, pillows and an eye mask. She guided us through a 30-minute relaxation with the gentle sounds of relaxation music playing softly in the background. I distinctly remember as I was walking slowly down the narrow staircase, steps I had run up on my way there, that somewhere deep inside of me said *This*. It actually said, *Not sure what that was, but **this***.

Yoga and meditation has been a huge part of my path. It has been my saviour, my friend and my ally in life. Yoga and meditation help me to reset, reconnect, ground and ultimately become freer.

UNDERSTANDING MY SPIRITUALITY

What does spirituality mean to you?

_____

_____

How can you take life less seriously? What would this look like for you?

_____

_____

Life is happening for you, not to you. Write your thoughts on this statement.

_____

_____

How can you better practise patience in your life?

_____

_____

'Being truthful.' What does this mean to you and how do you see truthfulness as a part of your life?

_____

_____

What is the greatest quality humans possess?

_____

_____

What does it mean to live in the present moment?

_____

_____

What are we all so afraid of?

_____

_____

Are we all one?

_____

_____

What do you take for granted?

_____

_____

CONTEMPLATE

IF PRAYING IS TALKING TO THE UNIVERSE, MEDITATION IS LISTENING.

MEDITATE FOR 20
MINUTES EACH DAY.
EXCEPT WHEN YOU
ARE REALLY BUSY.
THEN MEDITATE FOR
40 MINUTES.

– Zen proverb

MEDITATION AND YOGA

Meditation

Meditation is an elusive word. One thing is for sure, it's not easy. Of all the wellness practices it is the one that seems the easiest but is *always* the most challenging.

Sitting still, in silence, for any period of time might seem so simple that the benefits could be perceived as negligible. Yet what meditation does for the brain, the body and the entire nervous system is incomparable to anything else. Sitting still, in silence, for any period of time is a lot harder than it sounds. Our attention span is shortening and our capacity for mindfulness and total presence of mind is decreasing. Never before has meditation been more needed.

The writing is on the wall when it comes to meditation. Clinical, field and peer-reviewed studies have been done. It is used in schools, in prisons and on psychiatric wards. With modern medicine and machinery, we are able to scan the brain *and* the body in states of meditation and compare and contrast to normal states. A 2011 Harvard study revealed that an eight-week mindfulness meditation can actually change the structure of the brain by increasing cortical thickness in the hippocampus – the gland in our brain that controls learning and memory and that also affects how we regulate our emotions. What was also interesting is that the study showed a decrease in the size of the participants' amygdala, the part of the brain that is responsible for stress, anxiety and fear. (See https://www.ncbi.nlm.nih.gov/pmc/articles/PMC3004979/.)

So what exactly happens, and why is it so hard?

Simply put, meditation is listening. Listening really closely, with no distractions and with most of our senses turned off. Our attention is honed inward with no visual stimulus, no communication and no physical feedback. It is simply 'me' and the thoughts in 'my' head. With everything else pared back, there is nowhere to hide from these thoughts. This is the hard part. With no distractions we become bored. Restless. We want to stop and give up. Sitting still and in silence for any period is hard.

Fortunately, meditation is not an end goal, it is a practice. Like all things, it gets easier the more we do it. Learning to knit might not take us as long as learning to stand on our hands, yet both are possible if we continually work on it. In fact, committing to learning to stand on our hands may even be easier than committing to meditating every day!

The best way to start, like everything else, is to start *slowly*. Five minutes a day for someone who is not meditating already is a great place to start. And no matter what excuses we might find, we all have five minutes to spare. Start with five minutes every day for a month, then slowly increase the time.

How to meditate in three easy steps

I. Sit in a comfortable seat

This might be cross-legged on a cushion in the middle of your dedicated meditation space. It might be pulled off the road in your car with the phone turned off. We do the best we can with what we have. Yes, a clear space, a set time and a regular routine is optimal, but meditating whenever and wherever we can is better than not doing it at all. If we can give ourselves permission to allow things to look a little different to how we expect, we set ourselves up with the best chance possible to succeed.

2. Set a timer

A timer is a useful tool to keep us on track when we start. In the beginning, setting a timer helps the busy monkey mind as it knows the meditation won't last for ever! Your phone may have a gentle chime sound that will still function when the phone is on airplane mode. You might find that with consistent practice, and having increased your time, you no longer wish to use a timer. Allow that to happen as a natural and organic process.

3. Become aware

Become aware of your body and the sounds around you. The clothes touching your skin. Feel the places on your body that are in contact with the floor, the seat or the cushion. Notice where your hands are relative to your body. If you are inside, hear the sounds outside and notice any sounds inside the room. Feel your breath moving in and out of your body. These are all anchors and they are happening in the present moment. Be here in this moment, right now.

4. Mantra

Try using a simple mantra. Repeat this phrase silently in your mind:

As I inhale, I smile, as I exhale, I relax. When the mind wanders and goes off on its own, gently bring your attention back to the mantra. No judgement, no criticism. Kindly say to your mind, *Not now, thank you,* and return to the mantra. Set a gentle alarm for five minutes and continue until you hear it.

5. Awareness

Notice how you feel when you are finished. Take a moment to readjust, to move your body and to take in your surroundings. How do you feel compared to when you started? What is your mood? Your frame of thought? How do things seem around you? Taking some time to notice the effects of five minutes of calm will help to motivate you to return to this practice again and again.

Well done! You are now on your way to a daily meditation practice.

Yoga

Yoga means different things to different people. Even within the yoga community, each yoga practice looks different, *is* different and will represent something unique to everyone. There is slow yoga, hot and sweaty yoga, core-focused yoga, breath-focused yoga, yoga for veterans, yoga for runners, yoga that focuses on building strength, yoga that focuses on relaxation.

It's a very broad term and it's no wonder people outside of the yoga community have set ideas of what it's all about. The fact that it is a philosophy for living is far too ambiguous for most people to grasp – especially with the legging-wearing, skinny-white-girl branding being bandied around online.

So what is yoga?

Yoga is a holistic practice, meaning it operates from the perspective of the whole.

Simply put, it's a practice to connect body and mind. Think of it this way: in school we have neatly-divided subjects, science, maths, languages, arts. We also have physical education, a separate subject that focuses on our bodies while the others focus on our minds. We are raised to believe that body and mind are separate.

Body + mind + soul

This holistic philosophy teaches us that we cannot separate the two, body and mind, that they are fully interconnected. Practising yoga brings the two parts of us together. Through mindful movement with focus on our breath we come into alignment in body and mind. This not only helps us to feel more peaceful and relaxed, it allows us to connect with who we really are, a soul. Yoga is a spiritual practice and as such the journey of yoga is to become awakened to our true nature, which is so much more than this body and mind.

The process of moving the body together with a connection to our breath helps to purify our body in preparation for our spiritual awakening. It is a journey, an evolving process and over much time the practice of yoga develops and becomes a deeper journey within. One which helps to show us the truth of who we really are.

We can become very mind-focused and cut off from our body, which can lead to over-thinking, over-analysing and being constantly in the future or the past – and not in the moment. When we become disconnected to our body, we see it as 'other'. Sitting for hours on end at a desk doesn't help and an over-identification with the mind can lead to anxiety, sleeplessness and a lack of wellness.

We have these amazing, incredible bodies, they are our home and our vehicle through life. We are not separate to our body; our experience of this life is through our body *and* our mind. Unfortunately, the media has us fixed on the idea of a perfect body, something that in form doesn't exist. In fact, every single body is a perfect body.

HOW IS IT POSSIBLE THAT A BEING WITH SUCH SENSITIVE JEWELS AS THE EYES, SUCH ENCHANTED MUSICAL INSTRUMENTS AS THE EARS, AND SUCH FABULOUS ARABESQUE OF NERVES AS THE BRAIN CAN EXPERIENCE ITSELF ANYTHING LESS THAN A GOD?

– Alan Watts

And so we go about our day thinking up in our head about what we have going on in our lives. Feeling disconnected from our body. We may even find that where the mind isn't going becomes a grey place, beyond pain, somewhere we cannot access.

This is where yoga really helps. Yoga connects us to our body. And by connecting to our body we come out of the mind and into our body.

WE ARE NOT A MIND – WE HAVE A MIND.

WE ARE NOT A BODY – WE HAVE A BODY.

Our mind is a tool in the same way that our body is a tool. Yoga guides us inwards and connects us to our body. By doing that we connect to the present moment. In the present moment there can be no stress, no worry about a hypothetical situation that has not happened and that may not happen.

Yoga grounds us to the earth and pulls us out of our head. There are many other benefits. Our bodies are amazing, and they adapt so well to circumstance. If we sit in a hunched-forward position, day after day, year after year, our body will adapt: it will shorten the muscles on the front and weaken the muscles on the back so that it can adopt this position permanently. We need to balance our sedentary lifestyle.

Yoga, being a whole-body practice, moves the body in all its planes, backward, forward, side to side and twisting. Yoga works on flexibility. It addresses the spine in minute detail. It focuses on places that we don't have connection to, places where energy is weak and that can become tight and stiff. By moving with the breath, we bring our minds into our body, and through different types of movements we can create a higher sense of awareness and find peace in our mind and physical freedom of movement.

Yoga creates space in our body and space in our mind and in creating this space we are making room for a deeper sense of purpose.

BE GRATEFUL FOR YOUR BODY. IT IS THE GREATEST GIFT YOU WILL EVER RECEIVE.

* The carriage represents our body.

* The driver represents our mind.

* The horses represent our emotions.

* And the passenger represents our soul.

* For many of us, our carriage is in disrepair and is in need of attention.

* For many of us, our driver is drunk and operating carelessly.

* For many of us, our horses are wild and are totally out of control.

* And for many of us, our passenger is fast asleep, dreaming that she is a slave, when in fact she is a queen.

* We need to tidy up and repair our carriage.

* We need to sober up our driver and remind him that he works for us.

* We need to rein in our horses and learn to control them properly.

* And we need to wake up our sleeping passenger and remind her that she is a queen.

* While the carriage, the driver and the horses are all important for this journey, if it wasn't for the passenger, we wouldn't need any of it at all.

  – Indian parable

HAPPINESS IS
WHEN WHAT YOU
THINK, WHAT YOU
SAY AND WHAT
YOU DO ARE IN
HARMONY.

– Mahatma Gandhi

CREATE

Establish a regular meditation practice

There is an abundance of resources available on YouTube and as phone apps. My personal favourite way to meditate it to precede my quiet time with some deep breathing and to simply set an alarm for the time I wish to sit. I meditate daily for ten minutes minimum and sometimes longer. This is realistic for where I am at right now and works for me. Make a SMART goal for a daily meditation plan for you.

Give yoga a go!

If you've never practised before, consider signing up for a beginners' course. Do some research and find a great teacher.

If you've practised yoga before but have fallen off the wagon, consider signing back up for a class.

If you live in a remote place and don't have access to a yoga teacher, have a look online. You can find free classes on YouTube or get a monthly subscription to one of the many excellent yoga-teaching platforms out there.

If you practise yoga all the time – well done! I have no doubt that it is of massive benefit to you in your life.

MONTHLY REVIEW

What other practices can connect you to your spiritual nature?

_____

_____

_____

_____

_____

_____

_____

_____

How can you make time and space in your life for spiritual development?

_____

_____

_____

_____

_____

_____

_____

_____

MY NOTES

MY NOTES

MY NOTES

MY NOTES

MY NOTES

MY NOTES

MONTH TWELVE
Self-Love

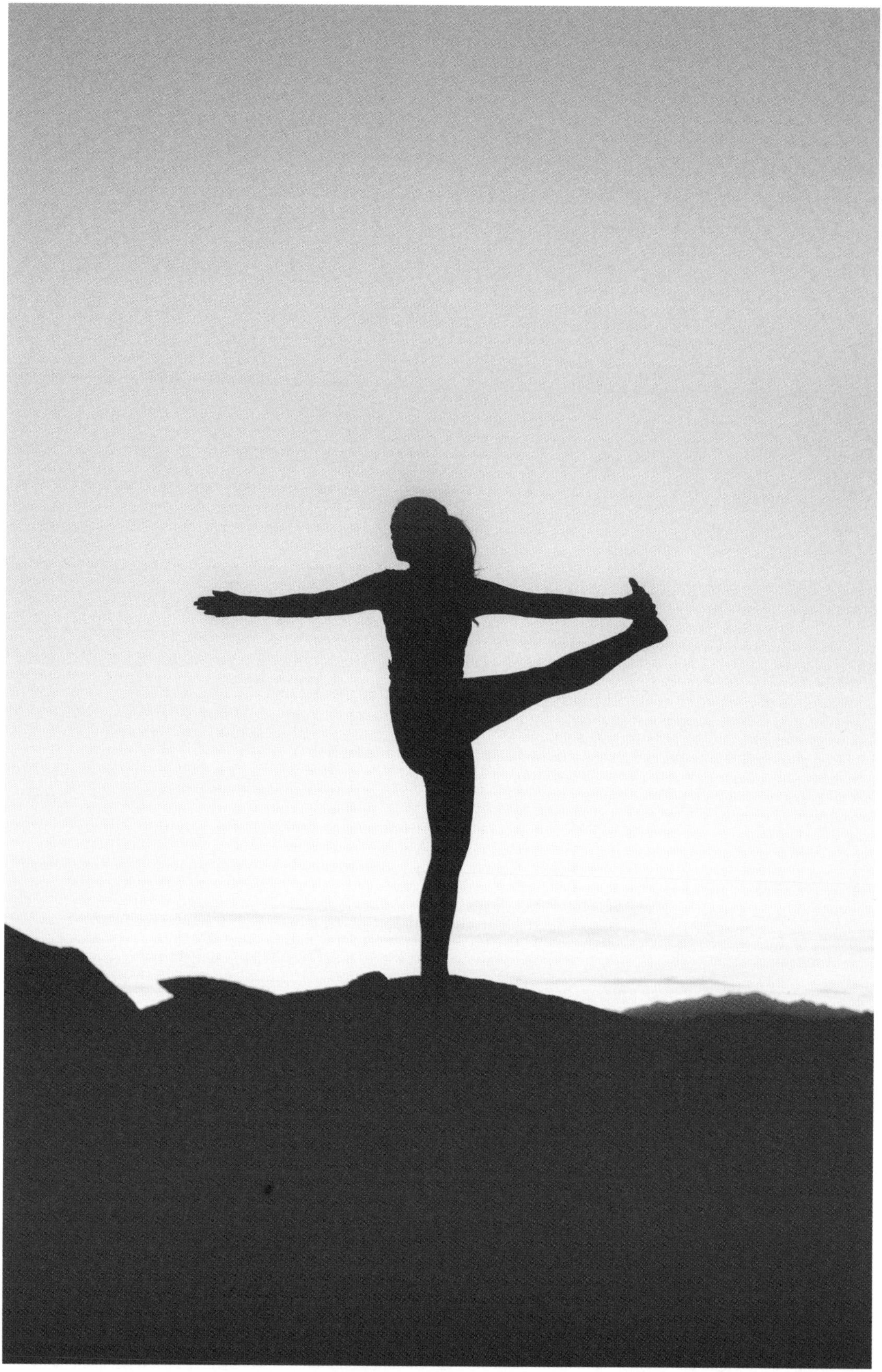

EXPLORE

We have reached the end of the year, well done for taking
this journey with me. I hope that it was rewarding and that the
process has allowed you to find some clarity on the direction you
want your life to move in.

This month we will explore self-love. We will also set intentions
for the next twelve months. Now is the time to think about what
you want to leave behind and what you want to create more
space for.

Anything is possible!

Self-love

I've left this section until the end because, being totally honest, self-love is a hard habit to build. For whatever reason, many of us have a self-deprecating inner critic, stemming from an 'I'm not good enough' core belief. Unravelling the reasons this core belief exists is a lifetime of work and will be different for everyone, but it is at the heart of why, for some of us, self-love is a challenge.

I AM ENOUGH.

I am enough.

I. Am. Enough.

The exercises in this chapter are possibly the most challenging – at least they were for me. I really recommend taking the whole month to write these series of letters and not rushing them. There is a lot of catharsis in this process. As these can be challenging and emotional to write, I really recommend using the listening partner exercise from Month One (p. 20). Finding someone you can talk to and share your experiences with or perhaps even your letter may be a really important part of helping you to process your words. Ensure that you set up the listening protocol so your partner knows they don't have to do anything other than hold space for you. If anything comes up in the process that you want to explore further, this is a great time to seek out a professional listening partner. When we are ready, healing will come. Knowing what we need is an important step in the journey. Asking for help takes the very strength and courage we are afraid of losing by asking for help.

Compose letters to your past and future self

This is a beautiful and challenging task that may bring up a lot of emotions. Opening a dialogue with ourselves and sending love, messages of support and encouragement is a powerful exercise. We may be used to being kind and loving to others but may not be used to issuing that same level of loving care to ourselves. Be as creative as you like and think of this activity as sending a lovely letter to a dear pen pal that they will hold on to and cherish for life.

* Write a letter to your seven-year-old self. What do you have to say to her? What advice can you give her about what is coming up for her in her life?

* Write a letter from your ninety-year-old self to your present-day self. What advice would your older self send you right now at this stage of your life?

CONTEMPLATE

Doing our best

We do the best we can with what we have. Our best might look different from day to day. When my children were very small, even taking five minutes to myself was hard. My best is different depending on how I'm feeling, how I slept and what my emotional landscape is. How I care for myself changes with the days and the seasons.

Life often throws us curve balls and it is at these times that self-love and self-care are the most important. Yet it is at these times that we often neglect ourselves the most, getting caught up in the trials and tribulations, the drama and the challenge.

Trusty tools for self-care

When things get tough, we need to recharge rather than continually outputting. Here are my suggestions on ways to generate more energy when you are finding life particularly challenging. I hope they are helpful for you.

Early nights – This is definitely easier done in the winter when the nights are long and the weather is cold but ensuring you get enough sleep is giving yourself the best opportunity possible. Rest is great too, so even getting into bed with a good book has wonderful benefits and reading before bed instead of watching something on a screen will set you up for a better night's sleep.

Baths – Twice a week I draw myself a hot bath with candles, Epsom salts, two pints of water and a good read (sometimes I treat myself to a Netflix binge, my laptop resting on my trusty IKEA step). My kids know this is sacred time and for the most part I am left alone! A 20-minute bath has been compared to one full sleep cycle. I always sleep like a baby after I've had a bath.

Walks – Taking time out to exercise, be in nature and breathe fresh air is good for body, mind and soul. Being in nature is restoring and walking is a gentle enough exercise to energise rather than deplete if you're feeling low. Doing this with a friend adds the benefits of companionship on top of all the others!

A night away in a hotel – Taking a break and getting away for a night alone is an amazing experience. The chance to do exactly what you want is a total tonic. Use it as an opportunity to replenish and get some you time in. Have a massage, steam and sauna, eat yummy food and sleep in a bed you didn't make. Heaven. You don't need to travel far if you don't want to, and there are budgets for everyone.

Breathing practice – Commit to a breathing practice. Knowing what it does for body and mind, making the effort to show up each day with this will bring you wonderful benefits. Follow your breathing session with ten minutes of meditation. You will be completely restored.

Yin yoga instead of physical yoga – I love my yoga practice and it's 'my' time. There is a physical style of yoga that I do several times a week with some friends and it keeps me going and is something to look forward to. On days when I'm struggling, my body can go through the motions – my muscles aren't any weaker but the practice required drawing energy from a well I knew was depleted and my instincts told me this wasn't a good idea.

I know sometimes there's nothing better to give us energy than to get the heart pumping, the body moving and to generate heat and sweat. But sometimes it's not what we need. Sometimes a slower, more restorative practice that quietens the mind, relaxes the body and charges the batteries is what is needed.

A massage or treatment – Take some time out for some body work. It's unfortunate that in our culture this is seen as pampering whereas in Asia, for example, it's a part of daily life. The power of loving, non-sexual touch is enormous and the benefits to both body and mind, not to mention nervous system, are not to be ignored. Think of it as maintenance, not a treat. We all need this type of self-care

Eating (mostly) healthily – When times are tough and stress levels are high, we might feel the desire to gorge on junk food or foods that make us happy in the short term. (I allow myself this momentary pleasure for two reasons: I know it is never as satisfying as I think it's going to be and I don't put these foods on a pedestal that I have to use willpower to avoid. This means I am always happy to move back to real food after.)

Eating lots of fruit, drinking plenty of water and herbal teas and making big, healthy vegetable soups are a big part of my emergency food when things get tough. I try to juice every morning and eat lots of oranges, apples, cucumbers, bananas, pomegranates, garlic and avocados in particular. Intermittent fasting also really helps to keep my energy banks full when things get tough.

No alcohol – When times are hard it can feel like a good blow out might shake the cobwebs off and be just what we need. Drinking is great in the moment but has short- and longer-term effects that can make a difficult situation harder, including bringing a lack of patience and more tiredness to the mix. In addition to making poor food choices, a hangover can lead to a discontinuity of the very survival routines that get us through these tough times, something we might be expecting the drink to do. It's a vicious circle.

Reflection

I went through a challenging period at the start of this year where for various reasons my load was doubled and pressure was high for a few months. What was interesting about this time was my increased awareness of being busy, being stressed and just how prevalent it seems to be around me.

These few months became somewhat of the proverbial straw that (almost) broke my back. Without caring for my needs and shifting focus to a self-care programme, I know my poor nervous system would have taken a hammering and implicated everything from my health to my relationships.

What I also observed is that this is life. Our situation can change at any time and we might find ourselves overloaded and overburdened. It has caused me to take a look at the responsibilities I do have and reassess whether my expectations of myself are reasonable or not. If one incident can almost tip me over the edge, perhaps my baseline is too high.

Maybe the low levels of everyday stress need to be rethought and restructured to make room for 'life' when it happens. Because it does happen. Perhaps it is our expectations of what we can handle and pull off each day that are really knackering our nervous system.

I wouldn't have said I was a particularly stressed person. I endeavour to manage what I carry with grace, ease and humour. Yet this situation taught me that my stress levels were literally just a hair's breadth beneath the safety line and any untoward situation could have put my health in danger. But the real issue is what is going on every day. Can our lifestyle support challenging scenarios when they happen? If we are like the camel, carrying our maximum load all the time, then we are not leaving any room for life's eventualities, for that extra straw.

We need to lighten our load now. Learn to prioritise our own health, our own stress levels, and our own well-being. Find a way that works for us that feels right and that is self-led. We need to love ourselves fiercely and with a sense of urgency. We need to start this immediately.

CREATE

Review Your Year

Celebrate your successes! Write about everything that you have achieved, everything that you have worked through and all the positive parts of this journey.

What did you learn? Explore the lessons you learned in the process of this book. How are you different now to how you were when you started? What was easy for you, what was challenging for you?

Reassess your intentions for the next year. As we complete this year cycle and you head into another, what are the areas of your life that you would like to focus on next? What would you like to create space for? How will you go about creating space, what do you need to leave behind you with the old year?

_____

_____

_____

_____

_____

_____

_____

Wheel of Life

Revisit the Wheel of Life on p. 15. When you are finished, compare it to the very first wheel you did when you started.

Answer the following questions.

What are the main differences between this wheel and the last wheel?

_____

_____

_____

_____

Where have you made the most progress?

_____

_____

_____

_____

In what areas of your life do you feel more balanced?

_____

_____

_____

_____

What are the areas of life you would like to focus on next?

_____

_____

_____

_____

What are the three biggest changes you want to make in your life over the next five years?

1. _____

2. _____

3. _____

Drawing from everything you have explored and reviewed in this book, write down some longer-term goals and intentions that you would like to focus on next year.

1. _____

2. _____

3. _____

4. _____

5. _____

6. _____

7. _____

8. _____

Epilogue

Well done on all your hard work. Taking the time for self-development is really important. When we make this effort, it doesn't just affect our own lives, it affects everything around us. As we grow more aware, it becomes self-perpetuating. It becomes a cycle. The growth doesn't stop until we reach the end of our road. The maturity, truthfulness and courage it takes to cultivate true awareness of ourselves becomes the baseline for who we are, how we see the world and what we will attract. We become more empathic, more loving and more open and can then hold space for these qualities to cultivate and grow in those around us. These are the qualities we need in our families, in our communities and in our leaders. These are the qualities that will lead the world forward in the direction of peace, equality and love.

MY NOTES

MY NOTES

MY NOTES

MY NOTES

MY NOTES

MY NOTES

MY NOTES

MY NOTES

MY NOTES